Journey to the Land of Promise

KATHY MATTHEWS

WESTBOW
PRESS®
A DIVISION OF THOMAS NELSON
& ZONDERVAN

WestBow Press books may be ordered through booksellers or by contacting:

WestBow Press
A Division of Thomas Nelson & Zondervan
1663 Liberty Drive
Bloomington, IN 47403
www.westbowpress.com
844-714-3454

ISBN: 978-1-6642-8060-1 (sc)
ISBN: 978-1-6642-8061-8 (hc)
ISBN: 978-1-6642-8059-5 (e)

Library of Congress Control Number: 2022918954

Print information available on the last page.

WestBow Press rev. date: 11/01/2022

Contents

Chapter 1

Journey to the Land of Promise

The Swahili word for promise is *ahadi*. Ahadi Empowerment Academy is the name of our ministry that God has entrusted us to operate. This is my journey to the Ahadi Land.

A Little Backstory

When I get to the end of my life, I want it to mean something. Isn't that what most of us want, especially as we age and start the second half of our lives? A divorce was the turning point in my life. It was pivotal. It changed everything, including the complete trajectory of what I thought my life would look like. Facing a major life change forced me to answer some very tough questions about myself. It gave me not only a new start but an entirely new blank canvas. I was forty-one years old, a mom of three grown sons, and working in the emergency department at the local hospital as a registered nurse. My life had suddenly become a train wreck. Once word of the divorce spread, my so-called good friends scattered, angry family members abandoned me, and what seemed like the whole town shunned me.

The place I called home was no longer my home. Life changed forever. Divorce changed everything about me: my view of life, my view of other people, my view of the church, and my view of God.

During that period, God's grace and love for me were the only lights I had left. I learned that unfaithfulness heals through brokenness. I was broken as never before, broken by life circumstances and in many ways by my own choices. I would like to blame my broken marriage on my ex-husband, like so many divorced women do. Instead, I take ownership. I was 50 percent of that marriage and 50 percent responsible for its failure.

I was married at nineteen, not fully aware of what I even wanted in life, much less what it meant to be a wife. I have always been a Christian. I accepted Jesus as a twelve-year-old little girl. I was raised in a God-fearing, Bible-believing, church-twice-on-Sunday, loving kind of home. Amid my train wreck of divorce, my priority was to get back on track with God. I needed my Savior. My storm-filled life and relationships were in shambles, and I felt I was being tossed around on the sea in waves of uncertainty. I needed the only anchor I knew: Jesus Christ. I knew without a doubt that, despite my messed-up life and broken relationships, God still loved me.

Romans 5:8 (TPT) says, "But Christ proves God's passionate love for us by dying in our place while we were still lost and ungodly."

I clung to that promise.

Another promise often shared with my growing sons and other young people was from Jeremiah 29:11 (NLT). But now I claimed it for myself. I would repeat it over and over: "For I know the plans I have for you, says the Lord. They are plans for good and not for disaster, to give you a future and a hope."

For several months following my divorce, my priority each morning was to remind myself of God's faithfulness, goodness, and love for me. Psalm 118:6–8 (NLT) says,

> The Lord is for me, so I will have no fear. What can mere people do to me? Yes, the Lord is for me; He will help me. I will look in triumph at those who

hate me. It is better to take refuge in the Lord than
to trust in people.

I tried to focus on God's purpose and calling over my life. At one
point, I wondered if there would ever be a day that I didn't cry. Day
after day, I felt broken. I felt like I was stomping around aimlessly
through mud—until one day there was a breakthrough, a sense of
purpose. God reminded me of my childhood dreams. I recalled the
call that God placed on my life years ago as a small girl. He wanted
me on the mission field. Somehow, someway, I knew it!

Being broken emotionally, spiritually, and physically does
something to your view of God's enormous love and unfathomable
grace. Like never before, I was grasping at a new understanding of who
God really is. He is so much more than the box we try to keep Him in
or the concept of who we *think* He is. A place of true humility and the
realization that you are nothing without Christ brings you to another
level. God is larger than this life. We can't possibly contain Him. He is
bigger than any battle and any sin. God picked me up and brought me
through all the hurt, grieving, anger, betrayal, and disappointment.

With God's orchestrating, I found new love, new friends, and a new
life. Best of all, I was obedient. Before 2007, I hated the word *obedient*.
It was like a noose around my neck or weights tied to my feet. I never
fathomed that true freedom was found in faithful obedience. No matter
what, I will, with every breath I have left on this earth, try to be obedient
to my Almighty Father. Obedience is where life is at. Obedience is where
true joy is found. Obedience is where peace is given. Obedience is where
wisdom and discernment are birthed. I am determined to be obedient
to God's calling on my life. There's a saying that reads as follows.

When you listen, God speaks.

When you obey, God acts.

When God acts, you change.

The passions He equipped me with for more than forty years were finally lining up with His purpose for my life. I could feel it, and I knew it. I no longer felt smothered. I no longer felt like I didn't belong. Obedience brings freedom like breath brings life. I finally understood my worth came from one source, which is Jesus Christ!

Nami. That's Swahili for "I am." I have learned that I am so many things through Jesus. I am loved, I am strong, I am gifted, I am enough, and I am a new creation. I am who God says I am.

I am chosen. John 15:16 (NLT) says, "You didn't choose me, I chose you!" You, my friends, are chosen!

This story is about God and His faithfulness. God can use anybody. Look at who God used throughout the Bible. I believe He prefers to use messed-up, broken individuals. We're the ones who know firsthand how desperately we need Him. While living in my cookie-cutter world, I had no idea how badly I needed God in my life. Nothing else and no one else—no home, no car, no job position, no title, no education—could ever fill the void that only God can fill. There's a hole in our hearts that only Jesus can fill.

Ephesians 1:23 (NLT) says, "And the church is his body, it is made full and complete by Christ who fills all things everywhere with himself."

Now you know a little bit of my back story and where I've come from. Maybe you can relate. Maybe you've come from a similar background. Hear me when I say *God can use you!* Your history doesn't matter. Your heart does!

Understanding takes time. Sometimes God uses other people to speak to you. A couple of years into my second marriage, I knew God was calling me into ministry—but I was afraid. I was holding back because I couldn't see a place in ministry for someone like me. You see, I was living with labels—the labels of "divorce" and "cheater." Shame is the Devil's game. Satan loves to give us labels, and he wants us to believe those labels are permanently stuck on us and define us. Jesus wants to rip those labels off! We are new creations in Him. Second Corinthians 5:17 (NLT) says, "This means that anyone who belongs to Christ, has become a new person. The old life is gone; a new life has begun."

God used a lady named Cindy to speak truth to me. She was the director of women's ministry at our church in southwest Florida. One day after attending a Bible study, Cindy wanted to talk to me alone. She asked me if I'd be interested in serving on the women's ministry board. My heart about jumped out of my chest. Of course I wanted to! I loved women's ministry. I loved encouraging and being around other broken women in need of the truth of who they are in Jesus. I loved sharing God's desires with other women. I loved loving on hurt women. Without any pause or prayer, I told her I couldn't.

That's right. I said no.

She urged me. She listed all her reasons for asking me. I told her that if she knew my history, and my labels, she'd think very differently.

With such loving encouragement, she asked if I would share my story with her.

I told her about my divorce. Boom! Strike one. Then I confessed that I had started another relationship before my divorce was finalized. Boom! Strike 2. And that led to adultery. Boom! *Big boom!* Strike 3!

I was waiting for her to say, "Oh wow. I was mistaken about you. You're right. You can't be in ministry." But she said words that changed the course of my life. She said, "That's exactly why we need you in ministry. Don't you see? God uses broken people unlike anyone else."

Hearing her words was like hearing from Jesus Himself. They were that powerful and true!

With uncontrolled tears, I received the truth and for the first time understood God's amazing grace. Jesus ripped off my labels and replaced them with His grace and love. I've come to learn that untested faith is a naïve faith. Until your faith has been under attack through various trials, it will remain immature and judgmental. You'll hold onto labels with an immature faith.

What Cindy taught me was a great truth. Understanding other people's perspectives and respecting them deepens when you have been battered and broken because of your own shortfalls and sins. Empathy grows out of a garden of brokenness.

Cindy then shared her own history, so similar to mine. It was unbelievable, yet amazingly true. God can and does use anybody. God will use you!

Chapter 2

Encouragement Fosters Empowerment

Ahadi *Empowerment* Academy

The growth and lessons I've learned in a lot of ways came from education, experiences, and encouragement. We've all heard that knowledge is power; well, I'd like to add and say that encouragement is empowerment. Education is empowerment. Empowerment is defined as the process of becoming stronger and more confident.

Over the course of your lifetime, can you think back to all those who impacted you and your future by encouraging you? In some cases, I believe it might be a discouraging word that can also impact our futures. Words are powerful.

In my life, my parents were both encouragers. They were my biggest cheerleaders. (Side note: just calling my dad a cheerleader makes me smile. When I was growing up, my father would tell me I could be anything I wanted, except a cheerleader. I never really figured out my dad's dislike of cheerleaders, besides not wanting me "dancing and jumping around" in front of a crowd.) My dad knew how much I liked to dance and how I loved gymnastics as a kid. My father was a sports fanatic. He loved any game that involved a ball. It was no surprise that he strongly encouraged me and my siblings to play sports. I grew up being a tomboy. There wasn't a lot of fanciness and frilliness in a neighborhood full of boys. I love sports. I love competition. A childhood of competing against boys in almost everything I did set the stage for raising three sons, and it also gave me the confidence to play against male or female in all of life's circumstances.

When I became involved in church ministry as a youth group leader, I was barely twenty. I led a group of eighth-grade thirteen-year-old girls. At that time, a woman named Sharon was working as the pastor's assistant. Sharon was a great encourager to me. She was my go-to gal for anything I needed involving youth group. I remember one time in particular when I wanted to teach a certain curriculum to my young ladies; however, it had lessons regarding sex and purity. I needed the approval of the board of elders and deacons to move forward. Prior to meeting with the church board, Sharon spoke the words of 1 Timothy 4:12 NLT over me:

> Don't let anyone think less of you because you are young. Be an example to all believers in what you say, in the way you live, in your love, your faith and your purity."

I don't recall exactly how things went down, other than I received my approval to teach the material. During this period of time, I saw how scripture could be lived out. Up to that point I had learned and studied scripture; now I saw the beauty of living it out and how it could guide me in my everyday living. Psalm 119:105 (NLT) says, "Your word is a lamp to guide my feet and light for my path." The Bible came to life for me while teaching those young girls. Sharon set the stage for that enlightening. Her encouraging words empowered me.

Later came Cindy, the lady who spoke truth to me in my early forties. Her words of encouragement lifted me into a deeper relationship and knowledge of God's character. To realize the power that words of encouragement hold is life changing. Encouraging words can literally change the course of your life. The awareness of female influence was becoming more and more clear. I deeply desired to be an encouraging influencer. I realized how powerful positive reinforcement and encouraging words could influence lives for Jesus. Cindy and her encouraging words again set the stage for my life's calling and ministry.

Cathy, who I call my sister-friend, was another woman who came alongside me and encouraged me when I needed it the most. God has a way of placing people in your life just when you need them. Look around you, and don't miss those people. Be aware of those people who are crossing your paths. I met Cathy on our field trip to Africa (you'll read about that later). Cathy is fifteen years my senior. I say that not to make fun; I say that to make this point. Ladies, God calls older women to be mentors to younger women. Be obedient to that, ask God to bring you someone to mentor or who can mentor you. These mentors, these older women, all played such an important role in my life, and pointed me in the right direction. Titus 2:4a (NTL) says, "These older women must train the younger women to love their husbands and children, to live wisely and be pure."

Cathy, my mature friend (I like calling her that), influenced and encouraged me in countless ways. One time in particular, my husband Mark and I were to meet with the pastors of our church during a tremulous time within the church. We were in the middle of a messy impending church split. Mark was asked to mediate a lot of the discussions and meetings and try to find mutual ground. We were on our way to another such meeting. While we were in the car, Cathy called me and said she had a word for me. She read Psalm 19:14 (NTL): "May the words of my mouth and the meditation of my heart be pleasing to you, O Lord, my rock and redeemer."

That piece of beautiful scripture played over and over in my mind throughout the entire meeting. I was so ready to spit fire. However, the Sword of the Spirit, God's words, kept me from saying something I would have later regretted. That scripture has been one of my favorites ever since. Through that church split, a lot of beautiful lifelong friendships emerged. One of those dear friendships was with another woman named Esther.

There are just some people who come into your life and instantly click with you. It's almost an immediate thing, a God connection and affection. Esther is a powerhouse of a woman. She has made it in a fierce business world, and has a passion for Jesus that is bold and commanding. Esther is one of those people who is a great influencer and encourager. I remember when she expressed her desire for us to form a charitable organization. With her prompting, Ahadi Empowerment Academy was registered and granted tax exempt status. She never once doubted it could be done. She serves as one of our board directors, and gives me wisdom and direction as needed.

Another time, I received a phone call from from Ochieng, our Operations Director in Kenya. He usually calls a couple times a week with updates from the field. This particular Saturday morning, he called while Esther was visiting our home, so Ochieng was placed on speaker phone as he gave me the report. The ministry had recently purchased a large egg incubator and he was calling to report how many eggs had successfully hatched. Sadly, out of the 300 eggs that were placed in the machine, only 120 produced chicks. We were disappointed, and the team on the ground in Kenya were feeling like they had failed. We listened to all the possible reasons why this may have happened, and what the experts said was the reason for low production. We were all feeling a little defeated and disappointed. Much to everyone's surprise, Esther was the first to say, "That's really good! Look at the valuable lesson you all learned: don't count your chickens before they are hatched. What a blessing those kind of lessons are." Such truth. Such wisdom. Such encouragement. This lesson also played a role when, a couple years later, we lost over forty pigs to an outbreak of the swine flu.

God wants us to look at disappointments as opportunities to grow and learn. All success comes with failures. God is to be praised in good times and bad times, in times of loss and times of gain. As we read in Job 1:21 (NIV), "Naked I came from my mother's womb, and naked I will depart. The Lord gave and Lord has taken away. May the name of the Lord be praised."

Esther isn't only my friend and mentor, she also is my accountability partner. She is a tax accountant, and numbers are her thing, especially when they are related to financial accountability. All good leaders have accountability partners. Time and time again, Esther has spoken truth to me. God has used her to affirm things I was praying about. He used her to answer my prayers about growing the ministry, when she had no idea I had ask God for direction. I love when He does that. Esther used Proverbs 29:18 (NIV to affirm what I had asked God for: "Where there is no revelation, people cast off restraint; but blessed is the one who heeds wisdom's instruction."

Esther has been and still is part of who I am and what Ahadi is today. She has shown me what it means to be brave in the face of great adversity. When God gives you a vision, you are not alone. He will give you the provisions you'll need to accomplish it. He will turn your vision into reality. He will use others to come alongside of you, encourage you, push you, pick you up, and cheer you on. Look for those mentors in your life. Ask God to place mentors in your life, and ask Him who you should be mentoring.

> May God, who gives this patience and encouragement, help you live in complete harmony with each other, as is fitting for followers of Christ Jesus. Then all of you can join together with one voice, giving praise and glory to God, the Father of our Lord Jesus Christ. (Romans 15:5–6 NTL)

Chapter 3

Looks Who's Coming to Dinner (1970 something)

~~~

Sunday dinner after church was a family tradition. Dinner usually consisted of baked chicken with livers, mashed potatoes, garden vegetables, and rolls. Throughout my entire childhood, we all sat down around the dinner table after morning church services and shared dinner as a family. The tradition continued years after we all got married and had children of our own. Every Sunday, we went to Mom and Dad's for dinner. Those are some precious memories.

I was the third of four children. I can still picture the dinner table and my assigned spot. I sat with my back to the windows, facing into the kitchen. My little brother Steve sat on one side and Mom on the other. Dad always sat at the head of the table, and my older siblings sat opposite Steve and me. I can still remember being told to clean our plates. This was quite difficult for me most days. I hated green vegetables (still do), and we had a lot of them at almost every meal. Dad made me sit at the table for hours after everyone was finished telling me I had to eat my veggies. He would tell me how kids in Africa were starving and I needed to eat what we were blessed with. I was obstinate and refused to eat something so hideous. I pleaded my case that God made me not like green vegetables and I should not be punished for something that was clearly God's fault. Mom would finally give in and let me go. I think Dad enjoyed seeing just how stubborn I was. I was never so thankful for a dog who would eat anything. I would sneak my veggies carefully under the table for the dog. My brother figured out a way to disguise his green veggies with a good slathering of BBQ sauce. To this day, he eats his green beans with BBQ sauce. It's funny the things you remember from childhood.

One Sunday, when I wasn't much older than six or eight years old, my father had invited a Nigerian pastor to join us. This pastor was in the States by invitation of a missionary woman at our church. Missionary Ruth was assigned to a community in Nigeria, Africa and traveled back and forth for years. That particular year, she brought back her friend the Nigerian pastor. During his stay in the States, a variety of church members invited him into their homes for dinner and fellowship. My father loved missions and he was more than excited to have this pastor share dinner with our family. I was awestruck. I was so fascinated by this man wearing a colorful robe with a matching stiff beanie-styled hat. His skin was so black that when he smiled, his teeth looked like flashlights. I wanted to know all about the world he came from. He was so intriguing.

That was when God planted the first seed of love for Africa in my heart. From then on, I asked for black baby dolls for birthdays and Christmas. I even received a black ventriloquist dummy named Lester; I had him for years. I watched anything I could on Africa, its people, and its animals. I loved watching *Wild Kingdom* on TV. I asked for *National Geographic* magazines, and loved to read and look at the pictures of all the different tribes of Africa. I was definitely hooked. I was in love with a place I had only been to in my dreams. How do you explain a deep love connection between a little white Dutch girl, from a midwest, middle class, conservative family and a foreign country and its people that she'd never met or experienced? Unbelievable, right? No—it was God. Isaiah 25:1 says, "Lord, you are my God; I will exalt you and praise your name, for in perfect faithfulness you have done wonderful things, things planned long ago."

A love for local and foreign missions had always been a part of our family. My dad was involved in a disaster relief and recovery group that traveled around the United States to help rebuild after natural disasters. He encouraged us to be involved in any mission-minded program that the church sponsored. When I was a small child, our family was involved in neighborhood outreach. Our church put on backyard Bible clubs during the summer months. In my teens, I started going on mission trips to other states. Our church youth group went to the Appalachian mountains of Kentucky through an organization called the Appalachian Reach Out. I loved those trips. To see and experience other people loving the same God as me fed my desires to learn about other cultures. It grew my love for missions.

As I grew, so did my desire, I wanted to experience other countries, and as a seventeen-year-old, I went to Haiti for a month with Youth for Christ. It was the first time I flew on an airplane. It was the first time I was in a different country. While in Haiti, we built a school and stayed in a bunk house with walls of only chicken wire separating us from the outside elements…and creatures. It was the first time I saw a cockroach; it was a big as a clothespin. Our team, divided into pairs, took turns staying up at night, in four-hour shifts, guarding our food supplies from the rats. Our restroom was a pit latrine. It was quite a different environment from my home in western Michigan.

I saw children sucking handfuls of mud from a puddle, trying to quench their intense thirst. The poverty was unreal yet so painfully real. We watched in horror as a women caught a stray cat, skinned it, and cooked it, so thankful and excited that she had dinner for her family. That experience changed my life. I knew God wanted me to help. I knew He wanted me on the mission field one day. He affirmed my desire to go to Africa by way of Haiti.

That was back in 1983. That was also the year I started dating my high school sweetheart, who three years later became my husband. My missionary plans were put on hold and replaced by a marriage and family plan. As my babies grew, I wanted them to share my love for missions. As they began school, I became a youth leader at church. Later, when they became teenagers, I helped to start a mission program at the church we attended. We did short-term mission trips to Jamaica and New Mexico, and were involved in a variety of local missions. I wanted my children to fall in love with sharing the gospel, and fall in love with other cultures. I wanted them to see the world beyond themselves, a world outside their little community.

As the boys got older, I went to nursing school, and began working in an emergency department. As the kids became more independent, the availability of financial resources increased. I found myself once again dreaming about going to Africa. I decided to start praying for an opportunity. I knew God would give me the desire of my heart if it was aligned with His will, as He promised in Psalm 37:4 (NLT): "Take delight in the Lord and He will give you your heart's desires." I was convinced that my desire to be a missionary was aligned with His will. I knew it would just be a matter of time.

Becoming a nurse meant more to me than just caring for others. Missionary Ruth from my childhood was also a nurse, and I wanted to do what she did. I was convinced God would use my medical experience to help on the mission field. God provided an opportunity. In 2006, I went on a medical mission trip to Kenya. On that mission, my purpose was made crystal clear. The seed that God had planted in me in the early 1970s finally became reality in 2006.

God spent over thirty years equipping me with life experiences, education, and training to prepare me for what He had planned next. If I have learned one thing in my fifty-plus years of life, it's that God's timing is perfect. It's never too early nor too late, it's always perfectly on time. Ecclesiastes 3:11 (NLT) says,

> Yet God made everything beautiful for its own time. He planted eternity in the human heart, but even so, people cannot see the whole scope of God's work from the beginning to the end.

God will use bad things as well as good things to accomplish His purpose for your life. To think God only uses good, positive events and experiences is foolishness. He uses *all* things to work together for His purposes. These include divorce, broken relationships, disease, and sometimes even death. He does what He needs to do in order to get you to the place He wants you to be. As we read in Romans 8:28 (NLT), "We know that God causes everything to work together for the good of those who love God and are called according to His purpose for them."

Chapter 4

Pokots and Polka Dots in 2006

Our mission team consisted of seven adults, including three nurses, two teachers, and two construction workers. We went to serve one of the more than forty tribes, the Pokot, in Kenya. They live in northwestern Kenya. What an experience. You become really close really quickly when you ride for three days on bumpy, dusty roads with nine others in a Land Rover meant for seven. You become really close really quickly when you all go potty in the bushes along the roadside. You become really close really quickly when you get to take turns hand washing each other's dirty laundry, polka dot underwear and all. You become really close really quickly when you hold parties celebrating a formed stool for your fellow team members. Yes, I just wrote about sharing personal bowel movements and celebrating them. Just keeping it real.

We were stationed with two American missionaries at a Mission base camp in a little village called Alale. The village was about three days drive, via Land Rovers, through tough terrain and dirt roads; I use the word *roads* loosely. The so-called road was more like what we would call a two-track trail. We used to drive Jeeps through the state game woods back home in Michigan on two-tracks, and the roads were sub-par to say the least.

The camp consisted of a small church, a landing airstrip, a school, and a medical clinic that was under construction. One day in particular stands out in my mind. It was the day the Doctors Without Borders helicopter landed on the airstrip. Later that day, an elderly Pokot man dressed in full tribal outfit stood guard in front of the helicopter. He stood on one leg, his left foot perched on his right knee, looking like a flamingo, and holding onto his walking stick. What a picture of contrast between worlds it was.

There were also a couple of small homes used to house the missionaries and some other staff members. Jen, a fellow nurse and good friend, was my roommate. We stayed in a small cinder block building consisting of three bedrooms. Each bedroom had a simple pair of twin beds covered with mosquito netting. We shared one room. The other two rooms housed a couple of guys from our group and a German helicopter pilot working for Doctors Without Borders. There was no electricity and no running water. Headlamps served as our only source of light. One night, Jen and I had gotten into our pajamas and untied the mosquito nets that are tied up in balls above the beds during the day. We each climbed into our tents of netting, ready to share about our day and have devotions. As I sat in my bed, encased by my netting, I pointed my headlamp over towards Jen seated in her netted bed. *Whoa!* I saw something move next to her. I calmly said, "What's that?" and pointed my headlamp next to her.

She looked down with her headlamp, and screamed at the top of her lungs. She was screaming, "Spider, spider, hairy spider!" I did the only thing any sane person would do: I screamed too and fought with my netting to get out of my bed and out of that room as quickly as humanly possible! The men came running to our assistance, acting all big and brave—especially after hearing it was just a spider. You can picture the eye rolls. How could we have been so riled up about a spider? Mind you, all we had in the pitch black darkness were our headlamps. The guys made their way into the room, searching as best they could with their lamps. Once they spotted the spider, they all screamed and gasped as well. It was a tarantula, about the size of mouse, all big and hairy. The thought makes me cringe even now, years later. One of guys eventually gained some courage and killed it with a shoe...yes a shoe...not pretty.

During our mission, Kenya was experiencing a deadly meningitis outbreak, and the World Health Organization (WHO) was sending helicopters into the mountainous regions to drop flyers about the disease and information regarding vaccination clinics in the surrounding areas. However, being that remote, very few people could read. The flyers were created using only pictures and moon-shapes to represent the days. It was the only form of communication, as there were no televisions or nor phone lines. It was *remote*. An old-fashioned ham radio was our only means of communication with the outside world. We were so out of place, but at the same time, I was so at home.

We spent our days working in the medical clinic. We treated case after case of malaria. We helped deliver a little baby boy, and we immunized over 2,500 men, women, and children with the meningitis vaccine. A couple of days were spent out on mobile medical clinics. We drove to very remote village churches. The driver stated peeping the horn about a half hour away from each church, alerting the people living in the bush that something was happening. They village people knew to go to the church when they heard horns. It was their way of communication with everyone else in the surrounding area. Our main focus at those mobile medical clinics was pregnant mommas and babies. We saw hundreds of pregnant mommas. We immunized and weighed countless newborns.

The things we experienced moved me in ways I can hardly put into words. We heard of the pregnant mother who spent five days walking trying to get to the clinic. She gave birth to one of the twins she was carrying along the way. That baby died and the momma had to bury her baby. Even so, she kept on walking, making her way to the health clinic, where she delivered the other twin, who survived. We watched another baby being born on the first night we arrived who was that momma's second child. Her first child died during the birthing process, which took place back at home in the bush. This time, along with her mother-in-law and husband, she walked while in labor to reach the clinic before successfully giving birth to a little boy. The labor process was nothing like how it's done in the States. The momma lay on a steel table lined with newspapers. She agreed to the needed episiotomy, which was performed with no pain killers. She gave birth. She never made a sound, not even a peep. Heavy breathing were the loudest sounds she made. After giving birth, she lay on the cement floor covered with a piece of thin material, nursing her baby. She was instructed to drink a vitamin-enriched concoction. Within a good three hours, she left carrying her baby, walking back to her home in the bush, which we were told was about a three-day walk.

We learned how many mommas and their unborn babies died during the birthing process due to the inability to deliver them properly. There is a tribal cultural tradition that many of the young girls unwillingly undergo, usually between the ages eight and twelve. It's female circumcision, also called Female Genital Mutilation (FGM). This practice is usually done by the elder women in the village. It is performed with sharp stones or pieces of metal. Many girls suffer horrible infections and life-long fistulas as a result of this non-sterile barbaric procedure. Different tribes have slightly different ways and practices. Kenya criminalized FGM in 2011, yet with many tribes, the practice persists because of deeply rooted cultural beliefs regarding marriage. When it comes time for these girls to give birth, the scar tissue has so distorted their birth canals and anatomies that birthing without an episiotomy becomes a death sentence for both the unborn baby and momma.

We also learned many babies die as a result of "cutting out the false teeth." Shortly after birth, the little white-looking spots on the bottom gum of the baby's mouth are cut out. This procedure results in infections and the lack of ability to nurse due to sore and painful mouths. Many newborns die. It felt cruel and inhumane listening to the stories and traditions. I was torn between screaming at the top of my lungs, asking how they could do these things, trying to understand these cultural practices that have been around for generations and are considered sacred traditions, and weeping for the girls and babies involved these practices. I realized the only way to break such a cultural cycle was education.

As we vaccinated, I saw how tough the skin of a man can be. Many of my sharp needles bent instead of puncturing the skin. With all my strength, I had to poke the men in order to penetrate their skin. One day, I watched in horror as a young child, maybe five or six, running around with bare feet, stopped, sat down, and with his teeth pull out a thorn, twice the size of a needle, from the bottom of his foot. He jumped right back up and continued playing. That would have been an emergency room visit for sure back in the States. We heard stories of little children having to be the ones to fetch water deep down in pitch-black small caves, because they were the only ones little enough to fit into the deep caverns. We witnessed grown adults fall to their knees, crying and begging us for our water bottles. I saw people rummage through our garbage that was meant to be burned, walk away with a gum wrapper or piece of plastic, and act like they just hit the lottery.

These people were tough and they were resilient in the face of incredible hardships. It was definitely a place where survival of the fittest existed. They were tough, emotionally and physically, yet they possessed a joy that was contagious, and they worshipped God in ways I had never seen. They had something that most Americans don't: they had a pure desperation and dependency on God. It moved my soul. I wanted what they had: to remove all the distractions and resources and enjoy utter and complete dependency on Jesus. Their faith taught me what completely trusting in God looked like. How many times have we sung the song "I Surrender All" and thought we knew what that meant. Until I saw what having nothing looked like,

I finally grasped what surrendering it all meant. We are so spoiled, my friends, but we are also so blessed.

My heart was "home," despite being on the other side of the world. The things I saw and the people I met changed me forever. The desperation for water was something I never could have imagined. The level of poverty tore through my being. The lack of resources, food, water, and even of civilization struck me at my core. How are these people surviving? Where was modern civilization, much less technology? Why wasn't this country doing anything to save these people? These questions just kept flooding my thoughts.

The culture shock I experienced was something I could have never been prepared for. It was almost paralyzing at first. I felt guilty for being in horrible shock at what I was witnessing. I felt guilty for thanking God I was born where I was. I felt guilty for *all* I had and had access to. It was emotionally overwhelming. The life of excess that I lived back in America felt wrong and shameful. I was overtaken with the need to help these people, these precious children, the girls, the mommas, the least of these. I can't help them all. Then, God revealed how I could help a few. Don't look at the big picture; look at the here and now. Look at who is standing in front of you right here, and right now. Start there, and then with a few more, and few more, and so on and so on. To believe the problem is too massive to make a difference, or to think that it's not your problem, or worse to ignore that this kind of poverty exists, are all just lies that Satan wants you to buy into. As we read in Zechariah 7:10 (NLT), "Do not oppress the widows orphans, foreigners and the poor. And do not scheme against each other."

Remember the promise of Proverbs 19:17 (NLT): "If you help the poor, you are lending to the Lord—He will repay you."

As an American, you will probably never know the level of hunger to the point of starvation and death. You'll never experience thirst to the point of dried cracked lips and tongues. We can, however, step outside ourselves and consider what must it be like not have medical help, to never experience school or any formal education, and to have no knowledge of technology or the outside world.

Stepping into the bush country of Kenya was like stepping back into a time when there was no electricity, no running water, not even a well that could be primed and pumped. There is no grocery store, no hospital, and no medicines. There are no shopping centers or restaurants. There are no books, there is no library, and there is no internet connection. It is a place where tribal traditions run deep and barbaric practices are still part of everyday life. It is a place where the children look after the grazing sheep and cows instead of go to school. It is a place where dowry still exists and child brides are common, and a place where little girls experience the horrific trauma of FGM. The list goes on and on of the hocking things we faced each day in the bush of Kenya. But somehow, in some strange way, I fell in love with the country and its people. I knew this was where God wanted me and I knew I was part of a much, much bigger plan, even though I hadn't a clue what it was. I knew God knew, and that's all that mattered.

Reentry back into normal American life is rough. Nothing feels right. I needed to figure out what to do with my feelings of guilt and abandonment. How fair was it that I was able to live in my comfortable, full-of-every-resource kind of life while so many were suffering? The answer was simple: I needed to do more, to give more, and to go again and again as long God provided the means to do so. Little did I know, I wouldn't be back until five years later. But God is faithful and I'll say it again: His timing is perfect. The feeling of being on the edge of something greater than myself never left me. I knew God had big plans for me, as in Jeremiah 29:11 (NLT): "'For I know the plans I have for you,' says the Lord, 'they are plans for good you and not for disaster, to give you a future and a hope.'"

Chapter 5

Life Happens

Relationships are messy, even when they're being well cared for. A relationship with no maintenance plan is just that: it's a plan of no maintenance, a plan for disaster. With no maintenance comes brokenness, disrepair, and dysfunctional pieces and parts. Things literally fall apart if they aren't maintained. Marriage isn't any different. It needs to be maintained in order to stay healthy. Married couples don't have to think alike, and should have individual dreams and ambitions; however, they should share mutual thoughts about their future. Their retirement plans should at least be on the same page.

Relationships are messy. Relationships that start when the people are teenagers have even more challenges because there's so much growing up that still needs to be done. In my first marriage, we had no maintenance plan, and extremely different retirement plans. We grew up and grew apart. God will use divorce. Beauty does come from ashes. So hang on—God will work it all out.

Empty nesters need to reconnect and rediscover a life without dependents. It's a new chapter, an awakening, so to speak, of new independence. You have to adjust back to just the two of you. What opportunities do you want to pursue? What do you want to accomplish in your lives? What does middle-age look like? These are all questions couples should talk about and answer together. Not everyone communicates. Not everyone likes to share ambitions and dreams. Some people want to just keep doing what they have always been doing. That is good enough. Some spend no time reflecting and no time contemplating, ignoring the changing life around them. Some people are just plain stuck in ruts that they've built for themselves and are totally comfortable staying there. I'm not one of those people. I hope you're not either.

I always thought I would have three different chapters in my Life. Chapter One would be childhood and growing up; Chapter Two would be marriage and raising children; and Chapter Three would be grandparenting and mission work. I had no retirement plan. I never bought into the "you're old now so retire" plan. I wanted to spend the second half of my life making a difference for the Kingdom of God. How many spend retirement in good health, indulging on themselves and family. I believe God grows you through time, experiences, and resources in order for you to use those tools and resources for His Kingdom when the time is right. Retirement is the right time. We have been equipped by the Kingdom for the Kingdom. We have to be Kingdom minded. Why else are we here? Those who can and those who are able should *go* and *do*! The great commission isn't just for those under sixty; it's for all of us until God calls us home. As long as you have breath, you have purpose on this earth. Whose purpose will you serve: your own or His? In the first chapter, I said that when I get to the end of my life I want it to mean something. Well now is the time to make your life mean something. You have the time and resources. Go and do. What are you waiting for? Be obedient. Prayerfully ask God what it is He wants you to do and where He wants you to go. Simply trust and obey.

I knew God had a calling on my life; that was clearly revealed to me during my first trip to Kenya. I wanted to serve the Lord on the mission field. However, my husband at that time strongly disagreed.

I think he thought I'd outgrow it, but how do you outgrow God's call? You can ignore His call, but you will never outgrow it, no matter how old you get.

After my divorce, I was ready to watch God take me somewhere else. No longer was I going to look at my present predicament as a setback. An uncertain present doesn't mean an uncertain future. It simply means God is still working things out for your good and His glory. I started looking at my uncertain present situation as an opportunity, as a way to engage with Christ on a deeper level. I needed to look full in His face and seek Him first above all else and above everyone else. From then on, I'd seek His plan, not mine. Isaiah 55:8 NIV says, "'For my thoughts are not your thoughts, neither are your ways my ways,' declares the Lord."

My beloved Mark. I met Mark before my divorce was finalized. It happened while I was on a vacation with some girlfriends. Something drew me to him. For the first six months, we communicated through emails and phone calls. He lived in a different state. However, timing is everything. Once word got out about my impending divorce, word also got out about my so-called relationship with Mark. That started the rumor mill, and put the finger pointing and assumptions into full swing. Hard, angry feelings were directed at me by close family members and friends. My world was turned upside down. I never knew people could be so judgmental, critical, and cruel. What hurt the most came from the people I loved the most. They had known me my whole life, and all of a sudden, they treated me as some kind of worthless adversary. No words can describe that type of betrayal.

There was no way to defend myself. People who only knew me as the baseball mom, or church member, or co-worker suddenly had horrible, hateful things to say about my character and my life choices. I thought many times how on God's green earth did people's opinions suddenly rise above any truth. Furthermore, where do these opinions come from, and what are they based on? Rumor? Gossip? Assumptions? Anyone who has been through divorce, or something less than stellar, knows what I'm talking about. People want someone to blame; they want to take sides. It's ugly and painful when you become the center of someone else's critical judgment. It hurts when your life is being judged, not based on truth but on opinion.

Christian brothers and sisters, it is not okay to gossip. It is not okay to judge. Critical spirits crush spirits. We must love each other. We must care for each other's wounds, not be the ones inflicting more punches. Leave your judgments for Judge. Your sin isn't any prettier than mine. God loves divorced people as much as He loves married people. God loves the sinner; He hates the sin, but the sinner He loves. My sin isn't any bigger than yours. We all fall short. No one deserves God's mercy, but yet He gives us abundant mercy every single day.

Lamentations 3:22–23 (NLT) says, "The faithful love of the Lord never ends! His mercies never cease. Great is His faithfulness; His mercies begin afresh each morning." Amen?

Unforgiveness takes prisoners. When you learn to forgive, the prisoner is set free, and that prisoner is you. God led me to a place where I just needed to love them, forgive them, and pray for them. God took away all the hurt and animosity once I understood the truth of Luke 6:28 (NLT), which says, "Bless those who curse you, pray for those who hurt you."

Mark wasn't a Christian. We talked for hours about Christ and faith. My relationship with Mark was one of friendship. We had an emotional connection, something I rarely experienced in my past. I saw early on the effects of alcohol addiction Mark was inflicted with. He was honest in sharing his struggle of addiction with me. It broke my heart and I began boldly praying for him. Mark was engaged to be married to another lady, but he was a mess. We spent hours talking on the phone, we emailed back and forth, I prayed with him, and talked to him about the amazing grace and love God has for each of us right where we're at. As Romans 5:8 (NIV) says, "But God demonstrates his own love for us in this: While we were still sinners, Christ died for us."

Mark had a hard time believing God could love someone like him, someone who had done the things he'd done. Mark needed God's grace, and know it was meant for him. God's grace is enough.

As time went on, I realized I was starting to have feelings for this guy, and decided that having feelings for a man who was engaged and an alcoholic was probably a very bad idea for me. I needed to end this thing before I felt anything deeper. I told him I wasn't able to be friends or communicate with him anymore. I wished him all the best and promised to continue to pray for him. Mark reluctantly agreed and honored my wishes.

Meanwhile, I continued working full-time, researching and talking with recruiters regarding traveling nurse positions. Over the next few months I started to narrow down my options; things were coming together.

However, God's plans were very different than mine. God knew Mark needed to be in my life and He made that happen with a series of bizarre and somewhat unbelievable events. Fast forward over the next few months, and Mark had a life-threatening internal bleeding episode that put him into a coma and in the intensive care unit. Upon regaining consciousness, Mark convinced his sister to contact me. I had never met his sister Becky, but she tracked me down and called me one day while I was at work. During that very awkward phone call, Becky begged me to come see Mark. She told me how he was in critical condition and He just wanted to see me. During those months of no contact, Mark apparently broke up with the fiancé.

I have to tell you: it wasn't an easy decision. I hadn't had any contact with Mark in a while—over four months. I did not want to get involved again. It was only through an act of God that brought me back into Mark's life. Mark's near-death experience was that act. I couldn't believe I was going to see him; it was purely God causing me to move. God gave me an overwhelming, undeniable urge to go see this man. I had *no* idea why, but I followed God's directing. I had learned to obey, even if things didn't make any sense. This was a critical life lesson. When we are obedient, God acts, and when God acts, people change.

Being deathly ill, hospitalized, and in a coma Mark to be led to the cross. Mark regained consciousness and professed his love for Christ. Mark knew God had saved him. Romans 6:6 says, "For we know that our old self was crucified with him so that the body ruled by sin might be done away with, that we should no longer be slaves to sin." That's when Mark saw first-hand the healing power of God.

Mark had been an alcoholic for several years, and he was still drinking heavily when I first met him. It was one of the reasons I kept my distance. Mark came to know the only way out of addiction was through Jesus Christ. Through Jesus, Mark has been clean and sober for over fifteen years. When the time was right, Mark and I got married. How wacky is that? God works in mysterious ways!

Chapter 6

Garbage Man to Ministry Man

A little back history on Mark.

Mark was one of four children of the Matthews family. His growing up years were spent in Indianapolis on the west side. The family home sat behind a couple of taverns and a liquor store on the banks of the White River. Mark spent most of his days playing with his older brother, Butch. The two would go fishing as often as they could. Mark tells of the times they caught carp in the river and then sold them to the neighbors as a way of raising a little money. Mark has a God-given gift of being a visionary; he is always looking for angles, and is definitely a way out of the box kind of thinker.

Mark's parents later moved the family to the outskirts of Indianapolis to a little city called Avon. It was here that Mark attended high school and played as many sports as allowed. As soon as Mark saved enough money, he bought a motorcycle—the first of many. Buying and selling was one of Mark's favorite things to do. He owned his first car at sixteen: a 1963 cherry red Chevy Impala. He bought his first Harley motorcycle while still in high school. Mark's father Ray worked at a local factory and ran a trash service on the side for additional income. Mark and his brothers all worked for the garbage business through high school. Mark recalls running a garbage route before school in the morning, and then having to go to class smelling like the job. Mark was either found on the back of a garbage truck, on the sports field, or driving one of his many vehicles or motorcycles.

After graduating from high school and spending a few years at Indiana University, Mark was hired as an ironworker. Mark traveled as much as money and time off allowed. Travel was a required part of work; Mark made the most out of his work-related travel by finding ways to explore, fish, or hunt in new places. Years went by and after numerous work-related adventures, Mark was called back to help with the family business.

A devastating car accident involving Mark's father and brother meant that Mark was needed to help run the trash service. After years of dedicated hard work and long hours, the trash service became one of the largest independently owned garbage companies in the United States. Mark worked tirelessly for the success of the family business alongside his younger brother Donnie and older sister Becky. Mark was not a Christian and led a lifestyle that resulted in many peculiar adventures, world travels, and failed relationships. Mark all the while had a sense that *something* was missing. When you don't have Christ in your life there is a void. A constant need for fulfillment, a desire for more, always searching for that *something*. God created humans to need Him. So many fail to see it's Christ they need. They go searching for that fulfillment in other things, things that bring escape, release, and satisfaction.

Mark's work experience grew him into a great salesman, and gave him the uncanny ability to talk to anyone. It also gave him a platform to wine and dine clients. Most evening hours were spent at sporting events, in arena club suites entertaining customers and suppliers. Mark's lifestyle was lavish. Mark's lifestyle was excessive and it was also physically destructive.

Not only was God grooming me, and equipping me, all those years, He was doing the same for Mark. Mark now uses all that sales experience and business knowledge to raise funds and market the ministry in a way that only Mark could do.

Chapter 7

Field Trip or Mission Trip?

Mark and I became involved in an incredible Baptist church in southwest Florida. We joined a connect group, and made some lifelong friends. In one of our small group meetings, I brought up my deep desire to go back to Africa, which Mark followed by bringing up his strong and deep desire to protect me. I shared with the group the calling I knew God placed on my life. Mark had been struggling with this topic. Mark wanted to support and encourage me in any way he could, with one exception: he did not want me to go to Africa. He refused to give me his blessing to go to Africa. He pleaded with me to go anywhere other than Africa. He thought Haiti would be much better, as it was much closer.

There was a lady in our small group named Frannie, a wise and godly lady. God used Frannie to affirm to me what I had already been thinking and feeling. If God wanted me to go to Africa, that's where I was going to go, no matter what anyone said, not even my husband. God used her to give me the courage I needed to stand up and be bold. I prayed fervently that God would bring an opportunity and make a way for me to go. I felt like young David facing a giant, as described in 1 Samuel 17:33 (NLT): "'Don't be ridiculous!' Saul replied. 'There's no way you can fight this Philistine and possibility win. You're only a boy, and he's been a man of war since his youth.'" If God made a way for David to defeat Goliath with a sling and a stone, surely He would find a way for me to return to Africa.

We had been living for a couple of years in Florida in a small condo. It was time we bought a home again, time to have something with plenty of room for our growing family. My oldest son Ben was married and had two sons; Tyler, my middle son, was soon getting married. God made it clear it was time to buy a place with space. We bought a home in the Smoky Mountains of Tennessee. We were told of an area church that was sending group of adults to Africa. We attended an informative meeting. After the meeting my husband and I were walking out to our car. Before I even had a chance to say anything, Mark said, "I think we should go to Africa!" I broke down and cried. God is a faithful God!

Our trip that time was an expensive one. Even to this day, I can't figure out how in the world they charged us such a price. We didn't know any better back then, and didn't even think about challenging the price. We felt we had been on a glorified international field trip. It felt like nothing more than an opportunity to pat ourselves on the back, check it off the good Christian bucket list, and say we went to help the least of these. Let me just stop and say this: if your motivation for going on a foreign mission trip is to check off a bucket list box, do yourself and everyone else a favor. Stay home.

We were less than impressed, and frankly very disheartened. Mark, in particular, was disenchanted with foreign missions. I, on the other hand, knew how a properly run ministry could be effective, Kingdom-impacting and God-honoring. My trip six years earlier to Kenya cost half the price for twice as much time in country.

Many ministries are run as businesses for profit. They can easily use well-intentioned people who desperately want to make a difference around the world, wanting to share Jesus with the least of these. Mark and I started a non-profit foundation, called One to One, upon our return from Africa. Our foundational goal was to vet foreign missions before a church would start sending teams to these foreign places on mission. We wanted to make sure what happened to us didn't happen to others.

However, God is God. He used One to One in a completely different way. He used the non-profit as a bridge church. Our church in Florida was going through a divisive church split. For over a year, One to One served a large number of displaced church members, and created a home church. We waited on God to show us a way forward. Would this church group officially become a new church? We explored different options, different meeting places, and different lead pastors. One to One served for a season in that capacity. It was a sweet time of growth. God wanted something different for Mark and me. One to One graciously dissolved two years later.

God provided another opportunity for us to get involved in foreign ministry. Through connections with friends, and friends of friends, we were put in touch with an orphanage in Kenya. God used our unfortunate international trip, and our connections through One to One, to bring us to Kenya. I can look back and see His leading from stepping stone to stepping stone. When God calls you to something, it's human nature to jump in head first, wanting to start things off with a bang. However, God seldom works that way. Instead of jumping into the deep head first, He wants us to just get our toes wet, and to wade in the shallow until He calls us deeper and deeper. It is His timing, not ours.

We became fully committed to the orphanage ministry in Kenya. Over the next three years while serving on its Board, raising funds, starting programs, and building walls and classrooms, red flags started hitting our radar. Again, we became disheartened. Story after story of questionable behavior unfolded. We spent three years trying to restore accountability. Unfortunately, we were met with excuses and resistance. No accountability was the root problem of that situation. The old saying that absolute power corrupts absolutely proved to be true. During our time in Kenya, we established many relationships and befriended many of the ministry staff. We cared deeply for them.

If you are thinking about sending a mission team, or donating funds, *research* the ministry first. Physically go to the properties, put boots on the ground, send a scout team first, talk to others, and ask questions of those who have personally been there or are personally involved. Put into action Matthew 10:16 (NLT): "'Look I am sending you out as sheep among wolves. So be as shrewd as snakes and as innocent as doves.'"

A wise and godly woman helped me understand that the battle was God's. We needed to move on, to let go and let God.

People want to believe what they want to believe; sometimes it doesn't matter what the truth is. We prayed and prayed for God to show us the way forward. Honestly, I walked away with a deeply wounded heart. Again, forgiveness was key. God taught me what it meant to pray for my enemies. I'd like to say it came easy, but that's not how it happened. Have you ever really, really disliked a person because of the pain and hurt he or she caused? Praying for the person seems absurd, right? However, Matthew 5:44 (NLT) says, "'But I say, love your enemies and pray for those who persecute you.'" Oh, it's so, so very difficult, but there it is—Jesus's words in the book of Matthew. I did it. I practically choked on my own words, and honestly didn't truly mean them when I first prayed that prayer. It took time. I knew it was what God wanted me to do. It was what I needed to do. Over and over, I prayed for that ministry and its leadership. I prayed God would restore it. I finally could honestly say I loved that ministry and forgiveness came.

I learned what it meant to focus on God and His truth rather than on the lies and rumors. It is so easy to get distracted with the drama of life. Satan loves to distract us from our callings, and distractions are one of his favorite ways to do just that. We learned to let God fight our battle, to turn the other cheek. I truly found the remarkable blessing in praying for my enemies. We learned the rewards of doing what is right are much greater than the consequences of with doing what feels good.

We certainly learned the hard way how *not* to do things in ministry. After this painful experience, I really thought about throwing in the towel. This couldn't be where God wanted me; there had to be something different. How could God keep wanting me to go through this pain time after time? Why would God give me a heart for missions, only to steer me straight into battles that ended badly? Did I hear God wrongly, was my heart's desire from my flesh and not from the Holy Spirit? *Or* was God training, teaching, and equipping me for something greater? These were all serious questions I asked God.

God used ministry after ministry to lead us to Ahadi Empowerment Academy. Can you see the thread of promise? God orchestrated every experience, good and bad. He wove it all together to create a beautiful tapestry.

Chapter 8

God You Make No Sense

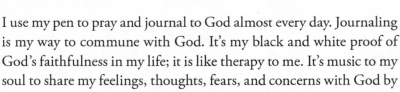

I use my pen to pray and journal to God almost every day. Journaling is my way to commune with God. It's my black and white proof of God's faithfulness in my life; it is like therapy to me. It's music to my soul to share my feelings, thoughts, fears, and concerns with God by writing to Him each morning. It's how I get into His presence daily. It's my way of memorizing scriptures. For some reason, I remember what I write down, so my journal is full of scriptures. God speaks to me through journaling.

In August of 2015, I was a journaling like a driven mad person. I couldn't get enough. We finally felt God release us from that particular ministry, and I was confused and hurt by everything that went down. As I was journaling one day, God compelled me write the words "You'll be running a school and ministry." Say what? Wait! What? I heard God tell me again and again, "You'll be running the school, and operating the ministry." That day in my journal I wrote these words: "God you make no sense!" I remember closing my journal and saying out loud, "No way, no how!" This could have been the end of my ministry story. However, there's something I've learned along my faith journey: when you're called to do something totally against anything you would have thought of, it's God! You better wake up and pay attention and truly wake up, even if you don't want to, even if you think God is irrational.

I was a mess for the next three days. I ignored what God had told me about ministry, and I continued to journal about other things. I felt miserable inside. My spirit was stirred and I was on edge. I knew God was right, go figure, and I knew I'd have to face what He was calling me to. I finally started to pray for clarity. I told God how confused I was. Why would He release me only to call me back into it? I begged God for clarity, and knew He'd reveal it to me.

During those few days, my sweet, observant husband, noticed I was off. Finally, he asked what was bothering me; he knew something was. He was right, and I shared with him my journal entry from a few days earlier. He took one look at me and said, "Well, He called you, not me. What are you going to do about it?" He had just reaffirmed that God called me. He also made it clear, he thought, that God didn't call him. Again, I was miffed. I prayed and journaled over the next several days for God's clarity on that particular matter. As Philippians 3:15 (NLT) says, "Let all who are spiritually mature agree on these things. If you disagree on some point, I believe God will make it plain to you."

Chapter 9

The Man on the Plane

Flying Delta has its perks, and I'm not talking about sky miles. Mark and I were remodeling an investment home in Florida that we intended on selling. We needed to travel back and forth from Tennessee to check on the progress and contractors every month or so. We booked exit row seating on this particular flight. It was the strangest arrangement I've ever seen. The exit row seats were configured three seats across, however, the seat by the window was facing backwards. It was foldable jump seat. I took the middle seat, and Mark sat on the aisle. "How awkward," I said to Mark. "I sure hope no one sits in that seat. They'll be staring right at us the whole time." We both started reading the magazines that we picked up in one of the airport gift shops. We were preparing to appear pre-occupied so not have to make small talk with whoever sat in that seat. A real Christ-like attitude, huh?

Doors closed, and I had a sigh of relief. No one had been assigned that funny backwards seat. Oops, I spoke too soon. A rather large-sized flight attendant stood next to Mark and said, "Excuse me sir, but that's my seat," as he pointed to the jump seat by the window. Really? Surely, his knees would be meeting mine as we sat face to face. Can you say *awkward*? He crawled his way passed us and took his seat. Yep, there it was. I felt the awkward stare as I kept my face in my magazine. That didn't work for long as this man was determined to get our attention and make conversation. He obviously didn't have a magazine to keep him busy. He complimented me on my necklace by saying, "Your necklace is beautiful. Whoever bought that for you must love you a whole bunch."

That comment got Mark's attention and Mark replied, "Yeah, and all I got was a fishing pole." That's all it took. They laughed and started a conversation that quickly turned into the most magnificent conversation I've ever had in my whole life. The flight attendant boldly stated that he could sense that Mark and I were spiritual people. Really? Okay...kinda weird, right? He said he could see that we were covered by the Holy Spirit. Okay...now, he was getting a little more serious. Mark asked him why he would say something like that.

He continued to tell us that since he was a teenager, he would receive promptings from the Holy Spirit to share things with people. Wait...what? He said when we walked down the aisle of his plane, he knew he had a message to give us. *What?* He said he had a message that was prompted by the Holy Spirit. Mark, sensing this was a bit strange, asked him if he was a Christian, and the man affirmed that he was. Mark, wanting more confirmation, asked him where he went to church.

The man replied, "Salem Baptist Church in Atlanta, Georgia." He then asked us if he could tell us something. He didn't want small talk; he was on a mission.

We said, "Of course." I was thinking to myself, *Who is this? And what is going on?* It was one of the strangest experiences of my entire life. The flight attendant then proceeded to tell Mark and me how we would be running a school in Kenya, and he described in detail the piece of property it would be on. Wait...what? How could that be? Who was this man? How did he know these things about us? We sat there stunned, speechless, and in total amazement. This man was confirming and clarifying exactly what God had planned for us, and in great detail. He was literally answering questions I had written days earlier in my journal. He told us that our school would need to be all on one campus. It would be overlooking a body of water. It needed to be fenced in. Then he said that we would not be partnering with who we thought. He asked if anything he was telling us was making any sense to us. You could see in his eyes the need for confirmation. I just shook my head yes, and started crying.

The flight attendant then got up and went about his flight responsibilities, leaving Mark and me sitting there, totally stunned and staring at each other. I asked, "Did that just happen? What is going on?"

Mark calmly responded, "He just told us how God's going to use us in Kenya."

I said, "Us? Did you just say us?"

Mark said, "Yep, looks like God has called me too."

I was speechless, and just cried. God most certainly did, and in a big way, a way so *big*, neither of us could deny it. *Wow!* Over the next hour or so in the air, I kept saying, "Did that just happen? How did he know all that? Was he real?"

Then, the flight attendant returned and sat down as we made our descent into Fort Myers. He asked us again if what he was telling us made sense to us.

I said, "Absolutely. You have no idea. I have been praying for clarity for days." I told him how God had spoken to me during my quiet time, while I was journaling. I told him how God told me that I would be running a school and managing a ministry in Kenya. I actually told God He was wrong. Obviously, I jumped to my own conclusions and was deeply conflicted. I wanted to be obedient, but it didn't make any sense in my mind. God had recently released us from a dysfunctional ministry in Kenya, and now He wanted us involved again? We were deeply hurt and financially burned, but it all made sense. God did not want us to be a part of that ministry;

He wanted us to run our own, and one that involves a school, but how? We were just blown away.

The man then said, "God will make it clear. He always does. He is faithful." *No* truer words were ever spoken. God is faithful. We never got the flight attendant's name. We just know he was a tall black man who spoke truth and prophesied over us. God used him to give Mark and me the message we so desperately needed to hear, a message of direction that we had been frantically praying for. We couldn't be more thankful that the flight attendant was obedient and told us exactly what we needed to hear to move us forward and fulfil our Kingdom purpose.

Can you imagine what that man must have been thinking to himself as he looked at Mark and me, knowing what message he needed to tell us? What courage! Anytime I start to doubt what we're doing or have fear we can't do it, I am taken back to that flight. I'm reminded of God's faithfulness and of God's plan for our lives. It's not my plan—it's God's. It's not my agenda or my ministry—it's God's.

Lead, follow, or get out of the way.

Pick your position. Where has God assigned you or placed you? What is your desire? Is it to lead, follow, or simply get out of the way? We have all been in one of those positions at one time or another. Depending on your circumstances and maybe your surroundings, you play a different role in each of those places. For instance, at work you may be one who needs to follow, but at home you are the one who does the leading. At work maybe you lead, but in church you follow, and in the world around you just stay out of the way.

I want to look more closely at what we should be doing and when we should be doing it.

My example is this.

God called me to lead this ministry, yet in many ways I follow Ochieng, our Operations Director's lead on day to day things and operations. When this ministry first started, I thought leading meant I was to make all the rules and decisions and control all the plans. We bought this property with the intention of opening an orphanage and school, however, God had other plans. He made it abundantly clear that I just needed to get out of His way, so much so that I wasn't even present for the ministry's grand opening. I was *not* needed there, but was needed elsewhere. God does not need me. I need Him. God doesn't need people to accomplish His plans; He allows us to be part of His plans. We are the ones who need Him, ever so desperately.

Do you have any examples in your life where you had to lead, or follow, or be out of the way?

Sometimes being obedient means to simply get out of God's way. In the case of this ministry, I just needed to open the gates and get out of the way. God controlled what this ministry has become. This is His plan, not mine. I take no credit, other than the fact I was obedient to God's call to own and manage a school in Kenya.

He will see to making it happen, whatever it is. He is the Author of our story; we're just along for the ride. We take things one day at a time and obediently do the next right thing. God has it all laid out, and He's guiding us on that path step by step. We don't have to know where the ministry is going, we just have to know who's doing the leading.

Psalm 143:8 (NIV) says, "Let the morning bring me word of your unfailing love, for I have put my trust in you. Show me the way I should go, for to you I entrust my life." This scripture is on a plaque attached to a huge boulder in our garden on the campus in Kikopey, Kenya.

From that time forward, we prayed boldly and fervently. We prayed for God's will to be done in and through our ministry. During this time, we were in contact with some of the staff employed by another American-based ministry, and learned that they were being treated poorly. We trusted God to change things for them, but were very cautious about getting too involved in the business of that ministry. We knew God wanted us to keep our distance and not interfere in any way with what was going on there. It was God's battle.

While on a college visit to Nashville with my son Tyler, I received a phone call from one of the board members of an American/Kenyan ministry. I was very guarded. The board member wanted to hear about our experiences with a particular Kenyan ministry. I felt compelled to be honest, but wanted to do it face to face rather than over the phone. I figured if she were really serious about hearing our ministry experiences, she'd set up a face-to-face meeting. A couple of weeks later, she came to our home and we talked for several hours. We shared stories, our hearts, and our love for the Kenyan people. She shared her interest in joining us in our new ministry.

Over the next few months, God named our new ministry by putting a song in my head. During my quiet time with the Lord, trying to think on a ministry name, there was a song that kept popping into my mind. It was "I am a Promise." It was a song from my childhood. You know how a song gets stuck in your head on repeat? If you've ever been to Disney and heard the song "It's a Small World," you know what I mean. Over and over the song kept playing in my mind as I sat in silence thinking about a name for our new ministry. That's it! The name needs to contain the word promise, and immediately I knew it was so. *Ahadi* means promise in Swahili. Based on God's promises to us, we created the non-profit ministry Ahadi Empowerment Academy.

Chapter 10

Cancer and God's Perfect Timing

We started by sharing our vision with close family and friends. They helped with the start-up financial support needed to launch our ministry. We needed to find staff and we needed to find land. Mark and I traveled to Kenya late in 2015 in search of property. We looked at several parcels of land. We visited several ministries as well, to get a feel for what others were doing. Our Kenyan-American friend, having family in Kenya, had some connections to land owners and we followed that path. We were looking in the Nakuru/Navasha area. Both areas had surrounding lakes. Much to our dismay, we came up empty handed. Either the properties were too expensive or too run down. We were feeling discouraged and, honestly, were desperate to find something before we went home.

That should have been our first warning. We should have known that these feelings were not from God. God is never rushed, desperate, or in a hurry. We got ahead of God and mistakenly took this project on by ourselves. Mark ended up making a deal with a property owner. We were thrilled and relieved, thinking we made a really sweet deal, not realizing we were being set up. In the coming months, after paying a substantial down payment, it was made clear to us that the property owner had no intentions of selling us his property after all. We backed out, and tried to recover our money, which the property owner still refused to give back. We had been burned, but we learned a *huge* lesson. We would *no* longer do things in our time, according to our agenda. We would wait patiently on the Lord, but goodness gracious, that is a hard lesson to learn. We committed our land search to God. We committed finding staff to Him as well. As Psalm 27:14 (NLT) says, "Wait patiently for the Lord. Be brave and courageous. Yes, wait patiently for the Lord."

The holidays came and went. We continued to pray for God's direction. In the spring of 2016, we heard that there might be a certain piece of land in Kikopey for sale. We couldn't get to Kenya until later that summer. We decided to wait and check it out then. If that was what God wanted for Ahadi, He would make it all work out. During that period of waiting, friends sent photos of the possible property back to us in the States. This particular property in Kikopey was situated high on top of a cliff bluff, overlooking a beautiful mountain range and Lake Elmenteita. It was "property overlooking water," just as the man on the plane explained to us. It looked perfect. We prayed about it and God confirmed that it was the property for us. God made it clear we needed to purchase this land. We obeyed, and agreed to purchase the property without ever seeing it in person.

After an intense due diligence of the title deed and survey, in October, my friends Sarah and Melanie and I made the trip to Kenya and signed the closing papers. Ahadi Empowerment Academy had land, a parcel that overlooks Lake Elmenteita. It was all God's doing, not our own. It was all in God's timing, not our own.

On this trip, God started to put our staff together as well. We decided to hire Benson because he had experience with American-operated ministries in Kenya. We had become close over the years and offered him a position. He introduced us to Ochieng, who God made clear also needed to be a part of Ahadi. Then Edwin, another Kenyan friend, introduced me to someone he said I needed to meet;

her name was Sarah. This woman moved my heart; I couldn't put it into words. When I met her the first time, I felt compelled to tell her, "I have a place for you!" I had no idea what that meant. We had just bought property on bare, dry, barren land. How could I have a place for her? I ignored the Holy Spirit's prompting, said nothing, and walked away knowing I had been disobedient.

Now for the cancer part. God is bigger than any cancer! One of the reasons I was unable to travel to Kenya sooner was that Mark had been diagnosed liver cancer in August of 2016. What first felt like a death sentence turned into a wonderful journey and blessing. God entrusted us with a cancer diagnosis. Mark had liver disease due to years of out-of-control drinking and Hepatitis C. He has been sober since 2007, the same year he came to know the Lord as his personal Savior. However, the damage had already been done to his liver. In 2012, Mark was miraculously chosen to be part of a research study group that involved a trial drug that cured Hepatitis C. Mark responded well and, after twelve weeks of treatment, he was free and clear of Hepatitis C. Praise God. Being free and clear of Hepatitis C meant Mark would have a better chance of receiving a liver if he ever needed one. We knew Mark was at high risk for liver cancer due to his liver disease.

At a doctor's visit in August of 2016, while I was on a vacation with girlfriends, Mark went to a routine follow-up appointment alone. He was told by a trusted liver specialist, that he had liver cancer. When Mark called to tell me, I simply didn't believe him. I was convinced that he heard the doctor wrong. After all, Mark had been known to get details mixed up. My husband knows me so well, and knew I wouldn't believe him. He asked our beloved liver doctor to call and tell me as well. Indeed, Dr. Schiff called me later that same evening. It was like a punch in the stomach. Suddenly my world was turned upside down. How could God have made our purpose so clear for ministry only to stop us with a cancer diagnosis? I was confused; I thought I heard God loud and clear, but now cancer? What made it even more painful was that Mark and I weren't even together. I was in North Carolina, and he was in Miami. The song "Thy Will" by Hilary Scott kept playing in my head. The words of that song spoke what was in my heart.

"Thy Will"

I'm so confused
I know I heard you loud and clear
So, I followed through
Somehow I ended up here
I don't wanna think
I may never understand
That my broken heart is a part of your plan
When I try to pray
All I've got is hurt and these four words
Thy will be done
Thy will be done
Thy will be done
I know you're good
But this don't feel good right now
And I know you think
Of things I could never think about
It's hard to count it all joy
Distracted by the noise
Just trying to make sense
Of all your promises
Sometimes I gotta stop
Remember that you're God
And I am not
So
Thy will be done.[1]

---

[1]   Hillary Scott and The Scott Family, "Thy Will," *Love Remains*, 2016, EMI Nashville and Capitol Nashville, CD.

This song played over and over in my mind. The words were the emotions and thoughts I couldn't put into words myself.

Still in North Carolina, before setting out on an early morning walk, I looked at my dear friend Michelle and said, "Why us and why now?"

She replied, "Why not you? Why not now?" With her answer ringing in my ears, I took off for a long walk on the beach. As I walked into the sunrise that morning, I remember yelling out loud at God. I'd like to say I was crying out to God, but I would be lying. I was mad; I was really, really angry. Our ministry was just starting to come together, I knew it was what God had planned for us, and I trusted Him. I trusted Him with His plan and purpose for my life, but I didn't like (trust) His timing.

I walked a long time first into the sunrise, the beauty of which irritated me. I turned my back on God's beauty and walked in the opposite direction. I cried, and spoke out loud to God. At some point my anger towards Him turned into a desperation for Him and I cried for help, a desperate cry to show me that He was still in control and that He was still faithful. I stopped and started to walk into the water up to my knees. That was when I looked up into the heavens and pleaded with God to show me His faithfulness. No matter what the outcome, I needed to know He would use it for my good and His glory. I remembered the man on the plane, remembered that he said Mark and I would be running the ministry. I asked God for a sign. I just needed a sign that everything would be okay, that Mark would be okay, that I'd be okay. I needed a sign in order to have a thankful and joyful heart despite this ugly news and impending scary journey.

With tears streaming down my cheeks, I turned around towards the shoreline and looked up at the random beach house just over the small sand dune. There it was: my sign, big as day! The address on the house was on a big sign that read in large numbers and letters 707 Signals. I ran out of the water and I fell to my knees. I started to smile, laugh, and cry all at the same time. God gave me the sign I desperately needed.

You see, 707 is what I call my "God number." It has shown up multiple times since I met Mark, and shows up when I need a reminder of God's goodness and God's faithfulness. Our random security code to our storage unit is 0707. Our address to the mountain house was 707 Laurel Top Way. I wake up many mornings at 7:07 a.m. The number appears on bills, in phone numbers, on receipts; it's the parcel number on the property that we owned in the Florida Keys. Over and over again, that number appears when I need the reminder of God's great faithfulness. It reminds me who God is. God gave me a sign.

From that time forward, I vowed to never doubt God's goodness and faithfulness. I knew without a shadow of doubt that whatever Mark's prognosis would be, I'd be okay, because I had a Father in Heaven who loved me and was with me, no matter what. God knows how thankful I became for Mark's cancer. It gave us a platform to share God's goodness and faithfulness with many, many people, including health care staff, as well as other patients and their families. If you were anywhere around Mark or me during his treatment, liver transplant, and recovery, there was *no* doubt who received *all* the glory. Praise God, Mark received a healthy new liver, and he has had no complications.

However, I can assure you if the prognosis had been different, God would have still been faithful and good, and His plans for me would have still been perfect. Mark and I both believed we were in a win-win situation. In life or in death, the victory is ours either way.

Prior to Mark's liver transplant, our home in the Florida Keys was devastated by Hurricane Irma, a category 4 hurricane that made landfall directly in the lower Florida Keys. Our home was on the "dirty" side of the eye, and our neighborhood was hit with multiple tornadoes. Many homes were completely blown apart; there was nothing left but rubble and foundations. Our home took a massive hit, but was still standing. We were faced with rebuilding at the same time Mark was actively on the liver transplant list, knowing we could get a call at any time. But, God is faithful and good even in the midst of a massive disastrous storm.

Our Kenyan staff came to the States to help us rebuild. What a blessing. For three months, they worked side by side with us and other contractors, rebuilding our island home. Ochieng, Edwin, and Benson worked, ate, and lived with us. God was building our relationships and bonds of trust with our ministry team as well as rebuilding our home. In all of God's sovereignty, two weeks after our home was completely rebuilt and once again livable, Mark received a call that a donor was found, and it was a perfect match for him. This was another lesson in how perfect God's timing really is. By the way, God isn't just bigger than cancer. He's bigger than any size hurricane, as Matthew 8:27b (NLT) says: "Even the winds and waves obey Him."

Chapter 11

Recovery and the Grand Opening

Recovery means a return to a normal state of health, mind, or strength. It is the action of regaining possession or control of something lost or stolen.

A grand opening is a special celebration held to mark the opening of a new business or place.

How do these two things go together you might ask? Well, it's exactly what was happening in our lives and in our ministry at the same time. Mark was recovering from his organ transplant at the same time Ahadi Empowerment Academy was kicking off its registration with a grand opening on the other side of the world. God orchestrated it to happen at the same time, which obviously meant Mark and I were not physically present at Ahadi's grand opening. Our great staff was ready and willing to put the party on without us. The most important thing was that God was present in both places: at Mark's recovery and Ahadi's grand opening. What more could we ask for?

Sarah. Remember I mentioned earlier that when I met this woman for the first time, the Holy Spirit prompted me to tell her we had a place for her? Well, on one of my visits back to Kenya, when

Mark was with me, we visited Sarah. I wanted Mark to meet her, and I needed to tell her we had a place for her. Sarah was running her own empowerment center for women when we met her, but was having a hard time paying the bills and was facing closing it all down. During that visit, Sarah invited us to her home. Mark had already made his mind up that she needed to be part of or ministry, and even extended her a love offering of $100, just because he felt compelled to do so.

Upon arriving at Sarah's house we met her husband Francis. They were people who loved Jesus. Sarah had no prior notice or warning that Mark and I would be paying her a visit. Once at her home, she shared how Mark answered her prayers. You see, Sarah was in a desperate situation financially and was praying that God needed to bring relief. I shared with Sarah what the Holy Spirit had placed on my heart. I told her we have a place for her. She sobbed. Sarah moved to Kikopey, into a little rental room, and went to work for Ahadi Empowerment. She started canvasing the community, promoting Ahadi and the upcoming grand opening. She shared what Ahadi Empowerment Academy intended to offer the community in classes and training for the women. She encouraged women of all ages to come and register at the grand opening event.

Based on Sarah's findings and the number of women who showed interest, our team was all set for the big day. Registration forms were ready. We purchased twelve chairs and two tables, and they were set up and ready. Drinks and food were ordered, and just needed to be picked up. We were ready. But God's plans are not our plans. His ways are not our ways. We were expecting a good dozen, maybe twenty women. God planned on over 500! Yes, I said over 500 ladies came through our gates. I'd like to say panic didn't set in, but that wouldn't be completely truthful.

Ochieng kept calling me and giving me updates. With every call, he confirmed more and more women. I wanted to give him words of wisdom, something encouraging, but all I could do was laugh. My socks were blessed right off! Women started to show up in waves. Sarah gave us her best estimate of how many ladies to expect. Twelve turned into over 500 plus. God made it clear, in a giant size way, that He hand-picked this ministry, this community, and these women. We had our job cut out for us.

When we stand firm on God's promises, we can all be world changers. We can all be influencers for Christ. We just have to trust God to be God. If you want your life to mean something, you must go and do something. Don't wait. Obey. Waiting to obey is disobedience. Go. As we read in Matthew 28:19 (NLT), "Therefore, go and make disciples of all the nations, baptizing them in the name of the Father, and the Son and Holy Spirit."

Chapter 12

Standing on the Promises of God

"Standing on the Promises of God" is our ministry tag line. One of my all-time favorite scripture verses is key to what we do. First Corinthians 16:14 (NLT) says, "Do everything with love." This is such an easy verse to memorize, but it can prove to be very difficult to implement. Yet, it's what we are called to do. All that we commit to do is run through this verse and this filter.

- Does it honor God?
- Is it in God's character?
- Is it Kingdom building?
- Does it fulfil one of God's promises?

From handling staff issues and students to proposing new programs and projects, everything runs through that filter of questions. If someone were to ask how we decide to do what we do, we reply it's simply obedience to God's call and the filter. I once heard a pastor say, "To be in God's will, you just have to do the next right thing." Why do we complicate God's will for our lives? Why do we spend countless hours on a treasure hunt so-to-speak searching for God's will for our lives? We just simply need to obey, trust God, and do the next right thing. By doing so, God's will, will be revealed.

> Trust in the Lord completely, and do not rely on your own opinions. With all your heart rely on Him to guide you, and He will lead you in every decision you make. Become intimate with Him in whatever you do, and He will lead you wherever you go. (Proverbs 3:5–6 TPT)

Getting into ministry and being its head used to scare me quite a bit. I really felt I was just too judgmental and critical of people. Sometimes I have a hard time loving everyone, especially those hard to love kind of people. You know who I am talking about, right? God pressed upon my heart that I needed to come super-duper clean and clear when it comes to loving people like Jesus does. I started praying consistently to love like Jesus and to lead like Jesus. I can testify that my love for people has grown enormously, not because of anything I've done, but because of what God has done in my heart and in my life. He has shown me true love, pure love, and unconditional love. I have learned to look at people, yes even the really difficult ones, through the lens of God's love. Scripture talks about how important love is, over and over. I sincerely want to love someone to Jesus. I want to love my way through anything. I've experienced a love that can restore and rebuild relationships that have been torn apart. It is a kind of love that can love Christ followers into being leaders for Christ. It is a love so powerful that it can turn the impossible into a possibility. I have personally felt the love of Jesus when I thought everything and everyone I loved dearly was forever lost. God's love restores and renews!

What Christ follower doesn't want to love like Christ? Have you ever wondered about loving like Jesus and what it really looks like?

Years ago, I was sitting in a small group of friends who were all believers. One of the ladies in the group started to share her experience with loving people—really loving them, and loving them like Jesus loves them. She said she had prayed for God to open up her heart and give her the ability to love others like Jesus loves them. She stated that God had answered her. He'd given her the heart to really love people. It's evident in her actions and how she lives her life. Her story stirred my heart. The Holy Spirit convicted me to pray that same prayer—not just pray for God to help me love others, but *really* to love others like Jesus loves them. I knew if I was going to be an authentic and genuine missionary, I needed to authentically and genuinely love people like Jesus does. I want a heart after God's own heart as in Matthew 6:21 (NIV): "For where your treasure is, there your heart will be also."

God is a change agent; He changed my heart and He can change yours. He made me more aware of *how* I was to love people, including people who like me, think and believe like me, know and love Jesus, and look like me as well as those who don't. The list goes on and on. The point is Jesus's love has no limits; His love has no boundaries.

For the mothers out there, have you ever thought you could ever love something more deeply than your own children? That kind of love is ginormous, massive, and pretty much indescribable. God gives us the capacity to love so fiercely and deeply. Whether your children are biologically yours or not, God gave you that motherly love for your child.

I met Wycliffe Ochieng Owino in 2015, but had heard about him two years prior to that. I first learned of him from the woman who ran an orphanage in Kenya. She told my husband and me about him, and said he came to live at the orphanage with his brothers and sisters after both of their parents passed. She told us he lived at the orphanage, graduated from the high school, and then moved away to take a truck driver's job in Saudi Arabia. No other details were ever given until years later.

God orchestrated seeing Ochieng. In 2014, I saw him face to face. We didn't speak, other than a greeting, but didn't really have the opportunity to do anything more. Frankly, he was acting very stand-offish. I remembered being puzzled by his behavior, but not giving it much thought other than that it was odd. Fast forward to our land search in late 2015. We spent time with a group, including Ochieng, for a couple of weeks while we scouted different properties. This time, we spoke in great detail. I listened to story after story of Ochieng's upbringing, his parents, and his siblings. I listened, many times with tears rolling down my cheeks, as he told me about the passing of his parents and what life was like living on the streets of Nairobi with his siblings.

His story touched my soul in a way I cannot put into words; even today I tear up trying to describe what God did to my heart when it comes to this young man. God made a supernatural heart love connection between Ochieng and me. I feel for him the same love I feel for my own sons. God orchestrated it all. God placed Ochieng in my life, and in our ministry. Mark feels much the same way regarding Ochieng. We are so proud of him and the man he has become. We have told him many times how proud his parents would be of him. One extra God bonus of Eternal Life is that I will get to meet Ochieng's momma, give her the biggest hug, and thank her.

We so respect the way he conducts himself and runs our ministry. He is our Operations Director. We truly believe we could have searched the world over and not found anyone any better or more suited for that role. We love his big heart. Ochieng runs hard after God's own heart. We thank God that, with everything that went all-so-wrong in Ochieng's young life, he turned to his Savior. He chose love and forgiveness, instead of hate and bitterness. He viewed difficult circumstances as opportunities. In many ways he chose life instead of death. Wycliffe Ochieng is the exception compared to other young adults whose childhoods were similar to his.

Chapter 13

The Ahadi Land

Our mission statement and goal are as follows.

> Ahadi Empowerment Academy exists to assist
> women of all ages, particularly young mothers,
> single mothers, and widows. We empower them
> with education and skills training, and provide them
> with the resources needed to achieve certification in
> a variety of areas.

> It is our goal to empower women to be contributing
> members of their communities, with a promising
> future for the generations that follow them.

Word about Ahadi Empowerment Academy spread like wildfire.
Who knew Kikopey had so many women? God. God knew the need
and He placed our ministry right in the middle of that need. God
was clearly marking His direction for our women's ministry. In fact,
He made it undeniably clear. He literally showed us the need.

On March 5, 2018, we kicked off our first empowerment classes.
We offered gardening, both in the greenhouse and outdoors. We
had sewing and tailoring classes, literacy training, Bible study, and

drama class. It was with great success that our classes took off. We currently offer training for about 100 women at a time. To date, June 2022, we've added several classes like advanced tailoring and sewing, English, Swahili, sales and marketing, evangelism, briquette production, and beauty and hairdressing, plus health classes and life skills classes. We plan to add computer training, catering, and hospitality classes as soon as funding is available. All classes are completely free to our students. It is our goal to have something for everyone, depending on their gifting and talents. We opened our Ahadi Health Clinic in 2021, and have plans to build a hospitality resort. To say God has shown His favor and blessing doesn't even seem to touch on His goodness. It just doesn't seem to say enough, but He is enough! He is enough!

Our Ahadi students commit to attendance and behavior standards that are God glorifying. Our students have a monthly community give-back day, which involves choosing a community project or community member who needs extra help and attention. The students collectively pool their giving and Ahadi Empowerment Academy matches their contributions. Then the ladies go to work. They have cooked and cleaned for a nearby orphanage. They have blessed an elderly grandmother caring for several handicapped children with a garden of her own, food, and clothing. They have helped a blind woman needing extra care and help with her housekeeping. They donated a bed with a mattress, pillows, and blankets to an eighty-two-year-old lady who had *never* experienced sleeping on anything other than the dirt floor. It's amazing how just a small gesture of love can change someone's outlook on life.

The idea of giving back planted the idea of what is now called our HOPE Care program. The letters are an acronym for Helping Others Prosper by Empowerment. This program carefully vets and researches the community of students, identifying those who are in most need of help. HOPE recipients are chosen very carefully through our vetting process. We take seriously the idea of giving a hand-up not a hand-out. This program has completely transformed many lives, and has restored hope to those who so desperately needed it to survive and face their situations. The recipients have a variety of needs, such as unpaid medical fees, electrical hookups, water tanks, seed for their gardens, school fees for their children, food and simple basic needs, as well new homes and rebuilt homes or help with monthly rental expenses. Through this program, we also help qualifying students launch their own businesses by providing scholarships for equipment and supplies to start up a new business. They are precious women of God, and we love them so much.

Chapter 14

It's Not All a Bed of Roses

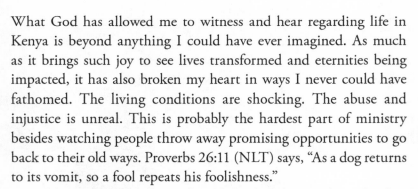

What God has allowed me to witness and hear regarding life in Kenya is beyond anything I could have ever imagined. As much as it brings such joy to see lives transformed and eternities being impacted, it has also broken my heart in ways I never could have fathomed. The living conditions are shocking. The abuse and injustice is unreal. This is probably the hardest part of ministry besides watching people throw away promising opportunities to go back to their old ways. Proverbs 26:11 (NLT) says, "As a dog returns to its vomit, so a fool repeats his foolishness."

The injustice, like I said, is unreal. As a mother of a law enforcement officer in the United States, I can say that some of our politicians, leaders, and American elitists need to spend time in a world where law and order doesn't exist. We'll see how long it takes them to change their rhetoric about defunding the police. Law and order exists for the highest paying bidder in rural Kenya. We had an instance where one of our pastors was terminated due to misconduct with female staff members. He, in turn, sought revenge and falsely accused one of our staff of kidnapping his own children (who openly confessed their father was lying) and selling them to me to traffic back in the States. Mind you, the area police arrested our staff member and wanted me (the supposed ringleader of the child trafficking ring) to pay $50 for her release. I refused and told them to arrest me instead, which the police chief refused to do. He insisted I leave the property. We had contacts higher up in government deal with this local police station and everyone was released without any bribes being paid. Later we found out the pastor who masterminded the whole story was beaten up for not paying his hired actors and witnesses.

Another time while Mark and I were in country and at Ahadi Empowerment Academy, a tribal clash broke out over cattle grazing rights; the fighting was happening right outside our gates. Spears and machetes were being used on opposing sides, while the police stood by and watched the fighting. Several men of one tribe jumped our then flimsy fence and attacked one of the innocent security guards with a machete. Mark and I were rushed to safety in a locked garage and inside of the locked Land Rover. Many people were injured throughout the community that day, and a number of them were killed. It was no laughing matter. I felt God's presence and protection in a very real way. While sitting in the darkness of the garage praying and pleading for God to intervene, the words of Romans 8:31 (NIV came to my mind: "What, then, shall we say in response to these things? If God is for us, who can be against us?" Just as Amos, one of our security guards, was cut deeply with a machete, one of the attackers started to yell, "These people are not our enemy!" They all jumped back over the fence and off our property. I truly believe God intervened at that moment.

In another incident, a six-year-old school girl in the community was attacked in board daylight while she was walking home from school, and was brutally raped in the bushes. No legal recourse was taken. The police did nothing to find the rapist, but later I heard that community mob justice took care of him.

Another story is of one of our students, a young mother whose husband was killed in a road accident. It is common practice for the husband's family to come and claim all of the husband's belongings, including his land and home. They have no regard for his widow or his children, and are tossed out on the street. This did not happen in this case. The other women at Ahadi heard this was taking place and ran to the aid of the young widow, again executing community mob justice. The student still occupies and owns her property. One of my goals is to teach the women that they are valued, they have rights, and they must stand together.

One day while Ochieng was repairing something outside our gates, a lady with a newborn child came up to him pleading for 100 shillings, the equivalent of ten cents. She was poorly kept, dusty and dirty, and the baby was the same. He asked her some questions and learned that her husband had been gone for three weeks looking for work in Nairobi, about three hours away, leaving her to fend for herself and child. They had nothing, except the baby was breastfeeding. Upon further investigation, the momma had a horrible case of mastitis, was barely producing milk, and was in severe pain. We were able to get her the food and the medical treatment she needed, plus we hired her husband as a night guard later on. There are no available government social services. I believe one of the reason so many don't help or turn a blind eye is because the poverty problem seems so overwhelming. As we read in Proverbs 31:20 (NIV), "She opens her arms to the poor and extends her hands to the needy."

How do you even begin to know where to help? You just start with what's in front of you. The injustice is gut-wrenching, horribly heart breaking, and often makes me wonder what in the world I am doing. But as quick as that thought hits my brain, I'm reminded of the man on the plane and I know I was born for such a time as this. God called me to this mission and ministry; He will lead me, guide me, and protect me in it. It's not all roses, it's not all blessings, but it is all so worth it.

One day, after sharing a lesson on Tamar and Jacob with the Ahadi students during a morning devotion time, I told the students that no matter what we've been through or what's been done to us, God sees us, we are valued by Him, we matter to Him, and He loves us. I asked the students if anyone wanted to give her heart to Jesus. Three students came forward that day. One shared some deep secrets about abortions. She stated she never knew or heard from anyone that Jesus could love even her. That, my friends, makes it worth it. As long as God gives me the ability, I will continue to do what He asks of me.

Our new Ahadi Health Clinic has improved the health of our staff and students. We offer a variety of services including STD testing, cancer screening, and hearing and vision testing. We are currently in the process of being fully licensed and certified as an HIV/AIDS testing and treatment center, which we'll open to the whole community. It's interesting to watch the students have health histories taken and exams done for the first time in their lives. Blood pressures are scary, and scales are foreign for many of them. It amazes me how they love learning about their health and take it so seriously, even taking notes any time we hold special health education classes. We've said it many times that they are like sponges, just soaking it all in.

Through our HOPE Care Fund, we have built nine new homes to date for community members. One home in particular has an emerald green door. I say that because she received her home shortly after my birthday one year. Mark had asked me what I wanted him to buy me for my birthday. I told him I've always wanted an emerald ring. As we were out looking and shopping for a beautiful ring, I received a request via my phone's messenger from Wycliffe Ochieng. He requested that a new home be built for a lady whose home was literally collapsing on top of her. She was a widow and a faithful student. He had gone to assess her concerns and he was shocked at the condition of her home. It was a mud hut, held together with branches and potato sacks. The roof was made of little pieces of trash plastic bags with rocks holding it all down. My heart broke at the photo he sent. Needless to say, I still don't have an emerald ring. However, Lona the widow received my birthday present: she has a home with an emerald green door. God constantly reminds me of all I have and of all so many don't have.

The trajectory of the Kikopey community is changing by empowering its women. Hope is being restored. Lives and eternities are being forever changed. God is eternally faithful and He is so forever good.

With the faithful support of our donors, we drilled a bore hole for a water well, even after being told there was no water in that area by the neighbors. We drilled down to 850 feet and finally hit water. It wasn't just a small aquifer; we hit a huge aquifer and were told by the drillers we would never run out of water. We serve the community of Kikopey by giving away clean and healthy water for free every other day. Water that was once a scarcity and would be a three to five mile hike away for most of the community was now basically available in their back yards.

We are also energy self-sufficient. We have solar panels that power our entire compound. Public electricity is available, but it is far from reliable. We have watched an entire area turn from desolate and dry into a thriving farm community. Small businesses continue to pop up throughout the community as well. Sometimes all you need is a little hope and little encouragement from others in order to bring new life. Hope is contagious! Hope is being restored.

Our goal at Ahadi Empowerment Academy is to be completely self-sustaining by the end of 2024. Our goal from the beginning has been to teach students to fish not to do the fishing for them. Far too often we have witnessed ministries fold up, retire, and even die right along with the founders and donors. It has been our mission goal to strive to build businesses alongside all the training and classes being offered at Ahadi Empowerment Academy. We have formed a for-profit business under the umbrella of the ministry leadership. Employees consist of graduated Ahadi students. After graduation, they are working, producing, and marketing a variety of goods through the various small businesses that have been opened. These businesses in turn help to fund the ministry.

Kipepeo Mrembo Enterprises is a division of Ahadi. We have a briquette company, community store, beauty salon, and full-service tailoring shop. God is growing these business ventures, and it is so fun and exciting to see the women successfully running them.

We have mission teams coming from the United States twice a year. One in the spring is focused on health clinics and health education; another in the fall is focused on the Annual Women's Conference that serves over 300 women from the surrounding community. There are many opportunities to get plugged in if God has stirred your heart to partner with us. There's a wealth of information on our website, www.ahadiacademy.org. As I wrap up this book, I want to thank you for taking the time to read my journey to Ahadi, and I pray that God has touched you to act on His call. If I can do it so can you. Nothing is impossible with Christ.

> Jesus looked at them and said, "'With man this is impossible, but with God all things are possible.'"
> (Matthew 19:26)

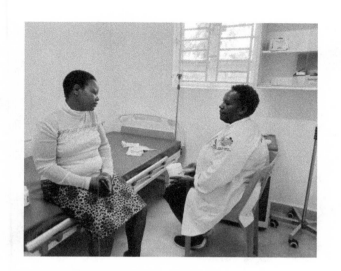

Official ribbon cutting

Chapter 15

Stories of Promises Fulfilled

Wycliffe Ochieng's Story

Life for John Owino and Rose Adhiambo was normal and ordinary by all standards in Eldoret, a major town in the Rift Valley, some 320 kilometers from Nairobi, the Kenyan administrative and commercial capital. They had seven children: two daughters and five sons (two of my brothers have since passed away). My father had formal employment as a technician at Ken-Knit Textile Company while my mother ran a small grocery business in our neighborhood. The aura of care and love could not escape the attention of our neighborhood that saw in them a resilient couple who wore faces of optimism in spite of the family putting up in a tiny one-roomed shack ambient enough to accommodate the family of seven. Two of my youngest siblings were born in Nairobi. My father's job was not well paying and, as result, the majority of my sibling were all born in our tiny, wooden, single-room house.

During those days, my mother would frequently tell us that being born in a hospital was a privilege. We lived in Eldoret in a small village called Elburgon. Five years after I was born, in 1992, my father, in search of a better life for us, took a job offer with a different textile company in Nairobi. After consulting with our mother, he decided to leave us in Eldoret. He travelled to Nairobi alone. My father would frequently write us letters just to check on us and ensure we were okay.

We used to attend a public school in Eldoret called Union Primary School. The school fees were between one and two dollars per child per term; at times, my parents couldn't afford to pay the school fees for all of us on time. As a result, we would occasionally miss going to school.

As children, we engaged in different games and many are the times that we would find ourselves in trouble with our mom. My brothers and I would leave the house at the crack of dawn and be back home when the sun melted like a lemon drop on the pink tongue of the sea. We would come back home so dirty after spending the whole day building toys using mud, and collecting plastics, old magazines, and bones and trading them for few shillings. My mom would beat us up because she was the one doing all our laundry.

Bad habits don't die easily. My desire to be a well-behaved, obedient boy was occasionally outweighed by the peer pressure from my friends. I thought of an idea of playing smart; I would sneak and join my playmates and, in the process, I would undress while playing only to put on the clean clothes every evening before going back home. My mom, the wide-awake woman that she was, took notice of the change. She began praising me to the extent of teasing my siblings .She would tell them, "See how Wycliffe has changed for the better."

It took her a long time before she found out what I was doing. Some of our neighbors used to tell her how some kids in the neighborhood were playing naked, a story that made her make fun out of without knowing that her son was the brains behind it. After close to six months since our dad had left for Nairobi; one day as a routine, we were collecting bones from the butchery in the market close to our home. I didn't know that my Dad had come to visit us from Nairobi, and worse still, he was in the butchery buying meat for us. I was in my birthday suit as usual when one of my friends shouted, *"Baba yako"* (your dad). The soul of skepticism was so awake in me that I thoughtlessly responded, "My dad is in Nairobi." I peeped through the butchery window and confirmed that indeed what I was being told was true. I ran home as fast as I could to avoid being seen by my dad. When I got home, I did not tell anyone what had happened.

As mom was preparing dinner, dad started telling her that the butcher had told him there were some young boys who collect bones and other discarded materials naked. Suddenly, I started having butterflies in my stomach because I knew my dad was going to give me a beating of a lifetime once he found out I was one of the boys walking around naked. Luckily, one of my brothers changed the topic, as everyone was very eager to hear dad tell stories about Nairobi. Three days after my dad's visit, he returned back to work with a promise that we would be joining him soon.

Two months after Dad left, a former colleague to my dad at Ken-Knit Textile Company came visiting one Saturday. I noticed him while he was still afar. In his hand, he had a brown envelope which my intuition told me was a letter from my dad. The nearer he got, the keener I became. He suddenly recognized me and called out my name. "Wycliffe, how have you been?" I respectfully replied that I was fine. He further inquired where my mom was, and I informed him that she was in the house. They chatted for a few minutes then I heard my mom shout, "God is great!" She had read the letter and the long-awaited news was finally here. Mom did not waste any time to break the sweet news to us.

"Ochieng," she began, "your dad has sent money for us to join him in Nairobi." I rushed outside and gave my siblings the good news. Everyone was jumping up and down because of excitement. Finally, we were going to Nairobi just as my dad had promised.

I started fantasizing how the food and water in Nairobi was not a match to what we were used to in Eldoret. I painted a very rosy picture of Nairobi. I imagined how different the streets and buildings in Nairobi were from the ones in Eldoret. The much-awaited day was here at last! We left Elburgon at 6.00 a.m. and arrived at the bus station in Eldoret at 7.45 a.m. on Saturday. We had with us a few bags that we had put all our belongings in, particularly clothes . At the bus station, shouts of Nairobi ranted the air; the more they shouted Nairobi, the more the picture was fine tuned in my mind.

At last Mom settled on Eldoret Express as the bus that would take us to Nairobi. Within four hours, we were in Nakuru. Out of excitement, I asked Mom whether we had reached Nairobi and she responded with a big *no*.

In less than three hours, we arrived in Nairobi. We were all in awe of the number of cars that we saw and the tall skyscrapers. When we got to the bus stop called Machakos Country Bus, it was a pale shadow of what we had earlier seen. The place was crowded, dirty, and full of hawkers selling a variety of goods. I spotted Dad talking with Mom through the bus window. He had come to pick us up using a company car. My dad's friend drove for roughly twenty minutes before we got to our new home, Umoja 1 estate.

The first assignment that my mother had was to identify a school that we would all join. It was not easy and this resulted in my siblings and I missing a few years of school. My mother wanted all of us to attend the same school and no school was willing to admit all of us at once. We lived in Umoja 1 estate from December of 1993 to January of 1995. Then we moved to another estate called Kayole, which is located about five kilometers away from Umoja. During the year of 1993, my mother gave birth to my brother, who unfortunately passed away after three months as a result of a lung infection. Later, in November 1996, my youngest sister was born at Pumwani Maternity Hospital.

In the year 1997, we joined a school called Edelvale Primary School that's located a few kilometers from Kayole. We attended this school up until my parents passed away. I must say life in Nairobi was not as easy as we had all expected. We would sometimes go for days without eating, because the amount that my father earned could hardly cater for all the bills as well as buy food for all of us every day. At least our parents' love kept us going.

I remember when we moved to Nairobi, one of my uncles, who is now deceased, came to live with us in our two-roomed house. He did not contribute in the family's daily expenses, but my father loved him and did not want to kick him out.

My mother was born with asthma, and at times she got really sick, especially when it was cold. I had to miss school some days so that I could take care of her. My three older siblings were always involved in other things. They hardly noticed our mother's condition gradually deteriorate.

In the year 2001 in the month of March, life took an unexpected turn when my father came back from work feeling unwell. His condition deteriorated so fast. We all felt so helpless since there was nothing we could do but watch his life being taken way. Those days, taxis were not a common thing, and emergency services here in Kenya don't work. In fact, we did not even have a phone to call my uncle and inform him what was happening. My father passed away lying in the bedroom. I later came to learn that my father died of meningitis. This is the time that I learnt how to distinguish true friends and those who pretended to be close to us when my father was still alive.

The days that followed were really tough for all of us. Losing a parent is really one of the most painful things that I have ever experienced. A few weeks later, we had to travel up country to a small town called Ugenya, a distance of 483 kilometers from Nairobi, to bury my dad. Three days after the burial, my mother decided that we should all return to Nairobi with one of my mum's friends so that we could continue going to school. She remained behind with my elder brother for a few more weeks as the African tradition demanded. When we arrived in Nairobi, we found our house empty.

All our belongings had been taken by our neighbors and relatives, who thought we were never coming back to Nairobi. We had not only lost our father—we basically had nothing except for the clothes on our bodies.

The death of my father really took a toll on my mother and her health deteriorated. Exactly one month after the death of my father, my mother passed away and we didn't even get to go to her burial because we came to know of her passing two months after she was buried. Those days, there were no phones. Our elder brother was the one who told us what had happened when he returned to Nairobi.

We had to move out of the house and live in the streets for seven months because we couldn't afford to pay the rent and none of our relatives was willing to accommodate us. Life became unbearable for us. We slept under semi-trucks and scavenged for food in trash cans. One day while we were roaming the streets of Kayole, we met with one of my other uncle,s who took us in. He used to live at Orbit, which by then was a construction company being run by an Asian. The orphanage had not yet been opened. There was just a primary school that was designed and build by the Orbit Construction Enterprises purposely to accommodate the kids of the workers at the construction company and the larger community that was around.

The primary school was being managed by an American missionary who used to visit the school frequently. On one of those trips, the need to start an orphanage was brought about. Around that time, we lived with my uncle in a tiny single room—all five of us—but it was better than sleeping outside in the cold. One day, my little sister was playing with some of her friends, and it happened that one of the missionaries was in town and he really wanted to know more about my younger sister.

I had just returned from fetching water when I heard some other children shouting "mzungu mzungu," which means a white person in English. When I turned around, I saw two white guys holding my sister's hand. I dropped the bucket very first and took off because I had never seen white guys up close. My elder brother welcomed them to the house and gave them a brief history about us. From there, the two Americans started bringing us food supplies while trying to find the best way to help us.

The orphanage was started towards the end of the year 2001; other kids were also taken in. While in the orphanage, I joined the church immediately since it was the mother church to the ministry. After my parents died, I had stopped going to church for a while because of what we had experienced at the Catholic Church. When my parents were still alive, my younger sister and I used to be devout Catholics; we never missed church. I served as an altar boy and my sister was an altar girl. Together we were so dedicated until the time that my dad passed away. The church that we diligently served couldn't offer any help to us during and after the burial. As a result, I opted to end my association with the Catholic Church.

As they say, time heals all wounds. I worked on my relationship with God, I got baptized at the Baptist church in the orphanage, and was given the name Andrew. I served as a youth pastor/leader in our church. During all this time, I was able to lead my fellow youths in different youth camps. Apart from the church, I started taking few roles at the orphanage; like being in charge of the boys' room. My duty was to ensure all the beds were well spread each day, the cleanliness of our school shoes and school uniforms, and also help with taking care of the young boys in the orphanage. At school, I was also the class prefect until I graduated from my primary level.

Life in the orphanage wasn't a bed of roses. At times, we used to be given hard labor as a form of punishment because of our love for football (soccer).

Our love for soccer would drive us sometimes to the soccer pitch during odd hours, and we would play against each other. We loved waking up at 4 a.m. while everyone was still asleep, and we would play soccer sometimes naked or in underwear. We really loved playing naked since it was so easy to maneuver around without anyone holding you by your clothes.

After completing primary school, I joined high school and while in form one, I dreamt about being in a ministry that was taking care of people from all parts of our country. When I woke up, I couldn't remember where all that was taking place; it seemed so surreal. God had given me a vision.

While still in school, I started working closely with the ministry's then manager who was so impressed with my work ethics and how I was handling everything at the orphanage and my schooling at the same time. He started mentoring me by trying to teach me how to drive and even how to use a computer. He kept on telling me that he was seeing a brighter future ahead. I couldn't figure out what he meant at the time and so, I kept on doing my best at everything that I was assigned to do.

Miraculously, one day our house manager was fired by the ministry's director. Since there was no one lined up to take over, I was asked by the director to help in managing the orphanage until we got the next house manager. Considering that I was just in form two (grade ten), that was so hard for me. But God was so faithful to me and without knowing, He was preparing me for a greater purpose. I kept on taking more duties in running the ministry affairs after the then project manager, who was also my mentor, got fired.

The ministry's director thought I was the right person to help in running the operations of the organization. At that time, I had not yet graduated from high school. I found myself most of the time trying to juggle in between my school work and trying to take care of my brothers and sisters in the orphanage, the staff and the mission teams that would come time and again. It wasn't an easy task, but the Lord was able to sail me through all that.

In the years 2007 and 2008, our country was going through the general election which didn't turn out well. It was marred with violence that left 180,000 to 600,000 displaced and 800 to 1,500 killed. The most affected people were slum dwellers. I led a team through the ministry to one of the slums called Mathare; we distributed vegetables and blankets, and secured the tents at the camp that were in bad shape due to the heavy rains that had affected our country at the time. It was a very painful experience. It was really hard for me to understand how easily people can turn against each other just because of an election. Through all that, the Lord led us in planting a church in the slum, which played a key role in helping the communities in healing and embracing love once again. I saw people who had killed and torched houses forgiving each other and preaching the gospel of Christ at the church and in their neighborhood. Later in the year 2008, I graduated from high school.

A year after graduating; things started taking a different turn in my life. The people that I had grown up and stayed with started turning against me. The person that I thought was like my parent started downgrading everything that I was doing. As I matured, and became an adult, I started seeing and understanding how things were being managed. I had asked questions that needed answers. It got to a point where everything I was doing was being termed useless. I shared what was going on with some of my friends. Some had experienced first-hand what I was going through. I had no choice but to persevere because I had nowhere else to live and getting a job in Kenya is almost next to impossible if you don't have a "god father."

I met Edwin, a co-worker, in the year 2011; the ministry's director had hired him as my replacement. Edwin was under strict instructions that he should never engage himself with me because, "I was possessed by satanic powers and I was rebellious." In reality, I knew too much. Edwin decided that the same person that he was told was satanic was the one that he was going to befriend. Since he had come to take over my work, we become good friends. He started doubting everything that he was told about me and he asked me if I could teach him the work that I was doing for the ministry. Without hesitation, I started teaching him and within no time he had learned everything.

One night in the year 2012 while I was preparing for my next day assignment, I was summoned in the middle of the night by the orphanage's director. I was told to vacate the house with immediate effect, citing that I wasn't respecting management or its property. I couldn't believe that it had come to that point. Once again I found myself homeless with nowhere to go.

Unlike when my mom and dad passed away, this time round at least I had made friends with caring people. Edwin and his wife really took good care of me through prayers and making sure I had food. I was staying with my other friend who had invited me to his house. I stayed with him for a few months. Through all that time, I kept trying to find a job until one day when I was introduced to an online site that was offering job opportunities in the Middle East. I applied for a sales and marketing job in Saudi Arabia. Mind you, I didn't have any background in sales and marketing. Luckily the company was hiring and training its own staff. My application was accepted and within no time my travel documents were ready.

I had met with Sharon, who is now my wife, at a Christian camp a few months earlier before I was terminated. She was about to start pursuing her bachelor's degree in public health. We kept on encouraging and praying for each other, hoping that one day the Lord would answer our prayers. I was off to Saudi Arabia: a new place, different culture, different people, different language, and different job. The first few months were so difficult for me and I kept on thinking should I continue working or go back home. I asked myself, "Where will I be going to and I don't have a place to call home back in Kenya." At this point I was being motivated by poverty; I did not want to end up being homeless again.

I started my job as a sales assistant and through the help of our Almighty God, in about a span of six months, I got promoted to a salesman position. The pay was much better, and I was able to take care of Sharon and my siblings. I worked in Saudi Arabia for about two and a half years, then I came back home and started working for a water company that is based in Molo Nakuru county as a sales representative.

Towards the end of the year 2015, I was introduced to Kathy and Mark Matthews. They shared their vision with me and that's how Ahadi Empowerment Academy was born. During that time, Sharon graduated from university in 2015 and she was having a very hard time finding a job. As a result, she had no choice but to volunteer at the Ministry of Health offices in Nairobi. After dating for close to eight years, we got married in the United States on 5 January 2019. Initially, we had thought of a simple wedding in Kenya with less people without knowing that God had other plans for us. God also blessed Sharon with a job at Ahadi Empowerment. She started working with us in February 2019 as the Director of Health Services. Then she took up the responsibility of co-heading the women empowerment department. She is an integral part of the ministry and I can't picture Ahadi without her.

When I met Kathy and Mark, they were sponsoring and taking care of three boys who were staying in the same orphanage that I grew up in. The three boys, together with the other kids, were being mistreated. At that time, we had not yet bought the land where Ahadi Empowerment sits today as the Lord was working behind the scene through all that. We kept on trying to find ways to help the boys, but all our attempts were being blocked by the orphanage administration. We managed to find a way to spend time with the three young teen boys. We took them out for supper. I can vividly remember that night how much the boys ate; it was like they hadn't eaten for a very long time. Being a product of the same orphanage, I related so well with what the boys were going through. It was so sad knowing that there were innocent donors out there giving their money towards the upkeep of these boys and someone somewhere was just pocketing all the donations.

> Do not take advantage of the widows or the fatherless. If you do and they cry out to me, I will certainly hear their cry. My anger will be aroused, and I will kill you with the sword; your wives will become widows and your children fatherless. (Exodus 22:22–24 NIV).

That night after the boys had finished eating, we took them back to the orphanage and started thinking how best we should deal with the whole situation. The director of the said orphanage had given orders that those boys should never be allowed to see their sponsors.

Knowing how Mark and Kathy really cared about these boys, we kept on doing our best in trying to help not only our three boys, but also the rest of the boys that were in the orphanage. One day, we attempted to take bags of food supplies to the orphanage and we were told they didn't want our help. We decided to deliver all the bags of food stuff to the District Children Officer (DCO) whose office was just nearby. The officer then placed a call to the orphanage and told them that there were some foodstuffs in their office that needed to be picked up. The orphanage administrator showed up and picked up the food supplies that we had brought. Once again that whole ordeal proved to us how hateful some people can be.

The boys were eventually moved, and are living in a safe and loving home to this day. They are attending school, and with God's grace will become contributing members to their society.

I look back through the journey that we had taken with these boys and I am just amazed how the Lord works through things. The boys are now happier, healthier, and well taken care of.

Ahadi Empowerment is a Christian-based organization that exists to assist women of all ages, particularly young mothers and widows. We provide them with love, care, theological classes, adult and literacy education, skill training, and employment opportunities. Our goal is to empower women to be contributing members of their communities, with a promising future for the generations to come. I am the field operations director and I oversee all the programs and projects being run at the ministry, manage all the staff members, oversee ministry funds and banking in Kenya, run weekly and monthly staff meetings, etc.

When we officially opened on February 5, 2018, we initially expected to have not more than twenty women show up to register for the various courses that we offer for free .We had purchased twenty plastic chairs. The women kept on streaming in and slowly we started running out of chairs. I was in charge of making sure we had enough seats. The more the women continued streaming in, the more I was running back and forth borrowing chairs from our neighbors. We were all overwhelmed by the number of women that kept on showing up. I had to call Kathy and inform her what was going on and, to my surprise, she started laughing at me.

By mid-day, we had registered over 500 women. At the time, we had only settled on starting with two courses: Biblical training and farming. The majority of these women had registered to take beauty and hairdressing, tailoring and catering, but at the time, we didn't have enough facilities to be able to train all the 500 women that had registered.

That day, they all went home proclaiming how the Lord had answered their prayers through Ahadi Empowerment. All this time, we didn't know that most of these women who had showed up were once displaced from their original homes from the 2007–2008 post-election violence (PEV) and they were all settled by the government in Gilgil, Kikopey area. As we continued serving them, some of them started opening up about their past and where they came from. It felt like the Lord was taking me back to where I started my journey when I was first serving the displaced people in Mathare, the second largest slum in Africa.

The Lord kept on blessing us as we kept on standing on his promises. Within no time, He provided the funds for building a chapel. Kathy, Mark, and the team from the United States were here for the dedication and once again the word of God came to me from 1 Samuel 7:12 (NIV): "Thus far the LORD has helped us."

Ahadi Empowerment kept on growing so fast, the programs that we had anticipated to accomplish towards the first phase of a five-year plan had started taking shape in a span of one year. Drilling the well wasn't something that we had thought would be done in our first year of serving the people of Kikopey. The Lord once again proved to us how faithful He is to us.

Those who hope in the LORD will renew their
strength. They will soar on wings like eagles; they
will run and not grow weary; they will walk and not
be faint. (Isaiah 40:31 NIV).

Before the well, the community around us used to walk for
about five to ten kilometers in search of clean water. Sometimes
they would go back to their houses without water. Most of them,
to date, have continued to share with us how Ahadi Empowerment
came at the right time for all the families around Kikopey. Under
the program Living Water, each family gets to fetch four buckets of
water three times a week.

Through the years, Ahadi Empowerment has continued to
register a tremendous growth in infrastructure and in empowering
hundreds of women in Kikopey and Gilgil respectively. Lives
are being changed. Lost hope is being restored through different
programs that we offer. The most hardworking students have already
secured job opportunities with us, and some are running their own
businesses. What started as a vision is today changing the lives of
the Kikopey community.

When I look back at my life and all that has happened so far, I
can't help but thank God as He has been faithful all through. I have
hope for tomorrow, and know that the days to come will be better
as we continue to faithfully serve Him.

Pricilla Mwangi's Story (Graduated Ahadi Student and Ahadi Project Manager)

I am Pricilla Mwangi, married to the love of my life Alex Maina.
We are blessed with three kids: Janty, Anthony, and Joyline (last
born). I have really seen God's grace throughout my life, having been
born from a very humble background. I got married at a very young
age without being financially stable, thus supporting my family was

a challenge. My husband and I really struggled to make ends meet, but it was all in vain.

I vividly remember borrowing money from my friend in order to start up a small business and fortunately God provided Ksh. 20,000 ($200) and I managed to start a cereal shop which brought in profits. I thought life was getting better. One fateful morning, I found out that thieves had broken into our shop and stolen everything. I was so devastated. I lost hope and became so stressed, though the word of God says that "all things work together for good." I was so frustrated, but above all life had to move on. I didn't allow any challenge to stop me from pushing ahead. I knew God had good plans for me. I was only left with Ksh. 1,500 ($15) on me. An idea came to my mind to start a grocery store and that was exactly what I did. Thanks to God it all went well.

At that time my first-born daughter Janty was in grade eight and she was about to sit for her final primary education examinations (K.C.P.E). My husband was jobless and the little money that I could raise from my store was divided to cater for food, house rent, clothing, school fees, debts, and so many other things. After my daughter completed her exams, I was to pick her up from school. The school was quite a distance, so I woke up early and took my leave. At around 11:00 a.m., I received a call from my neighbor that my house was on fire! I was so confused. A day that had started well ended up in a terrible way. I will live to remember 5 November 2016; it's the day I lost everything. On the other hand, I was five months pregnant with my last born. I had endless questions, like "Why me?" "Am I cursed?" and "What had I really done to deserve all these?" Because of my spiritual strength and how I grew up trusting in God, I didn't lose hope. I didn't give up though I was helpless. The word of God came to me saying, "Come to me all who labor and have heavy burden and I will give you rest." This verse gave me strength to move on.

Friends and family contributed what they had to us. We were forced to move from Nakuru Town to Kikopey in Gilgil. Life was unbearable, being in a new place where we know no one. The place was dry with no water, and my husband and I were still jobless. It was just so hard I cannot even get enough words to explain the miserable state we were in. When I was about to give birth, my husband was forced to look for job in order to cater for our needs. God was always on our side; we never lacked anything. In March 2017, I gave birth and I thank God it all went well though challenges were still there.

I came to learn about Ahadi in April 2018. It is not far away from where I live—just a walking distance. I heard that they were helping women. I decided to visit the institution where I found someone who explained to me what Ahadi was all about. I took a course on organic farming, which is under Project Green Thumb. After graduating, I continued coming to work at the farm and helping out in Project Kuku. By the grace of God, I got employed in May 2019. It was a great opportunity to serve in the ministry.

Being in Ahadi has changed my life in a great way, spiritually, socially, and financially. I also have achievements that I have gained through Ahadi. I bought a water storage tank that I have been dreaming of for a long time. I'm also grateful that I can also support my husband in providing for our family. I am looking forward to continuing encouraging other women to get empowered, to realize their potential, and make use of their available resources to generate income, and to keep them informed of the word of God and trusting in Him, not to rely on their own thoughts.

Glory and honor to the most high God for this for in His own time he made everything beautiful. He is God of promises. His promise is *yes* and *amen!*

Purity Wanjiku's Story (Ahadi Graduate and Kipepeo Mrembo Storekeeper)

My name is Purity Wanjiku, second born out of five siblings. I am a born-again Christian. Jesus is my personal savior; he is my protection and guide in my life. I was brought up in central Kenya in Muranga County. I started to help my mother on some of her duties like selling kales and onions so that we could get our daily bread.

My education ended at form four. I was not able to further my education because of the challenges in the family. After the final national examination (K.C.S.E), I went to live with my cousin in Muranga town. It was really interesting to change life from living in the village to living in town. In my thoughts, I knew that I was going to get a job, start earning, and help my mother. My cousin told me that she could help me find a job, so I used to stay back at her house looking after her kids. I came to realize that she wasn't interested with finding me a job; instead, she just wanted me to continue with the duties I was helping her with at her house. She was just wasting my time.

I started looking for a computer school where I could learn more. I shared the idea with my dad, and he was willing to support me with the fees. My cousin wasn't happy about this. She told me to take evening classes so that I could remain home handling duties and taking care of kids. I didn't argue with her, hoping that one day things would be fine.

After two months, I was done with computer lessons. My worry was going to back to being idle at home. I started waking up early every morning, taking care of all house duties, then going out to look for a job. God's favor was upon me. I found a job in a shop where I was assigned to be cleaning and arranging products. I was being paid Ksh. 100 ($1) per day, working from 7.00 a.m. to 7.00.p.m.

I decided to move out of my cousin's place and rented a house. The house was not in a good condition. It used to flood whenever it rained.

After several months of struggling, while looking for a better paying job, my mom connected me with her friend who was a manager in a hotel in Naivasha town. I was taken in on June 2013 and they started training me on the job which was to take six months. I was training in fields like housekeeping, receptionist work, and kitchen services. The hotel took care of everything that I needed. I appreciated the offer. God was answering my prayers.

In the housekeeping department, I met a friend, Amos, who was very kind to me and ready to help me in whatever duty I was assigned. I kept wondering why he was this much friendly and kind to me.

Three months later, the guy started proposing to me. I didn't like it because I thought he wanted to take advantage of me. He didn't give up, even after I was done with training. He kept in touch, but I never engaged back. A few weeks later, I decided to give him a chance and all worked out perfectly. He is now my husband and father to my daughter.

After the training, we were to start the job but unfortunately things turned out negatively. The operations and human resource manager called all the trainees, about fifteen of us, and told us that our period being there was over, and we would not proceed. We were just given recommendation letters and transport to take us back home.

Three weeks later after staying at home, my friend called me and asked if I could work in a small café as a waiter. The owner of the café was to offer accommodation and food. I was okay with it and accepted the offer. Working there became difficult because of the working hours and also the food was not being provided very well. I later quit the job after three weeks.

During Easter season, something crossed my mind that where I was training might be busy. I went back there to try my luck. Luckily it went well, and I was taken in. I started working and I was being paid Ksh. 500 ($5) per day. After that Easter season, the head chef said that the number of chefs was low. Luckily, I was given a chance to interview. There were many other people set for the interview, but I was not afraid of anything because I trusted in God and believed that He would do it all for me.

The interview time took too long; that made others to lose hope in waiting and leave. It later happened that they never conducted the interview but gave us a chance to work. We were given a three-month contract, and after those three months I was employed permanently. Three years later, they started delaying salary and it became hard to survive. On the other hand, I was three months pregnant. Amos and I decided to quit the job so that we could find other ways that we could sustain ourselves together with our unborn child. We went to Amos's home (his parents' home). His parents never liked me because of my physical appearance, but my husband didn't leave. I kept on praying that my parents-in-law would one day accept me and love me as their daughter.

We struggled very hard to get household items and other things to sustain us. Due to that, I developed high blood pressure, even after giving birth to my daughter Ivy. I was not able to see her because of pressure.

We later moved out from my parents-in-law's home to our own place, though we still struggled on ways of meeting our daily needs. The new environment had its challenges; the place was dry and with no water. I had to go look for water a far distance, carrying my daughter on my back, and even carrying her while going to casual works.

Four months later, Ahadi Empowerment Academy was offering courses to women who were interested. I went on and registered for a bead work and beauty course. I took the bead work course seriously knowing that it would later help me one day. I later took a poultry course headed by Mr. Ochieng as the teacher. He was so friendly to us students and also kept encouraging us about life, sharing his life experiences with us, until I came to accept situation the way it was.

I kept praying that one day I and my husband would finally get a better job. During morning devotion prayers at Ahadi, I took a step of faith and wrote a prayer request about it. God works in His own ways. Ahadi needed a daytime security guard and my husband was given that opportunity. We really appreciated God's miracles and we were happy for the answered prayer.

God never fails those who trust in Him. We kept our faith in Him and few weeks later, Ahadi management called me to their office and offered me a job opportunity in taking care of the chickens.

I am so grateful that God answered my prayers. He responded to me in His own ways. I lift His name high. I am now working at Ahadi, a place where the foundation is the word of God. The management is so caring to everyone regardless of who you are, what you look like, or where you come from. I have seen the hand of God and experienced His love throughout my life. May the name of the Lord be praised and bless Ahadi for everything. Glory be to God.

Bibliography

Scott, Hillary, and The Scott Family. "Thy Will." *Love Remains.* 2016. EMI Nashville and Capitol Nashville. CD.